THE JEWISH QUARTERLY

The Jewish Quarterly is published four times a year
by The Jewish Quarterly Pty Ltd
Publisher: Morry Schwartz

ISBN 9781922517142 E-ISBN 9781743822739
ISSN 0449010X E-ISSN 23262516

ALL RIGHTS RESERVED.
No part of this publication may be reproduced, stored in a retrieval system or transmitted in any form by any means electronic, mechanical, photocopying, recording or otherwise without the prior consent of the publishers.

Essays, reviews and correspondence © retained by the authors

Subscriptions 1 year print & digital (4 issues): £42 GBP | $56 USD.
1 year digital only: £25 GBP | $32 USD. Payment may be made
by Mastercard or Visa. Payment includes postage and handling.

Subscribe online at jewishquarterly.com or email subscribe@jewishquarterly.com
Correspondence should be addressed to: The Editor, The Jewish Quarterly,
22–24 Northumberland Street, Collingwood VIC 3066 Australia
Phone +61 3 9486 0288 Email enquiries@jewishquarterly.com

The Jewish Quarterly is published under licence from the
Jewish Literary Trust Limited, which exercises a governance function.

UK Company Number: 01189861. UK Charity Commission Number: 268589.

Directors of the Jewish Literary Trust: Lance Blackstone (chair),
John Cohen, Andrew Renton and Michael Strelitz.

Founding Editor: Jacob Sonntag.

Editor: Jonathan Pearlman. Associate Editor: Jo Rosenberg. Literary Editor: Natasha Lehrer. Sales and Marketing Coordinator: Therese Hava. Management: Elisabeth Young. Design: John Warwicker and Tristan Main. Production: Marilyn de Castro. Typesetting: Tristan Main.

Issue 250, November 2022
THE JEWISH QUARTERLY

Contributors   iv

Nir Baram (translated by Jessica Cohen)
Amos Oz and A.B. Yehoshua: A tale of political twins   1

Arik Glasner (translated by Jessica Cohen)
After the prophets: The next generation of Israeli writers   35

History
Steven Nadler The curse on Spinoza   53

Community
Michael Vatikiotis A community to celebrate:
The Jews of Singapore   61

Reviews
Irris Makler Inside the Old City of Jerusalem   67

Benjamin Balint Jacob's ladder   77

Catherine Taylor The unforgettable worlds
of Natalia Ginzburg   87

Contributors

Benjamin Balint is the author of *Kafka's Last Trial*. His next book, *Bruno Schulz: An Artist, a Murder, and the Hijacking of History*, will be published in April.

Nir Baram is an award-winning Israeli author and journalist. His latest novel is *World Shadow*.

Jessica Cohen has translated leading Israeli writers. Her translation of David Grossman's *A Horse Walks Into a Bar* won the Man Booker International Prize in 2017, and she is a Guggenheim Fellow.

Arik Glasner has published two novels, *And at This Season* and *Why I Do Not Write*, and a book of literary criticism, *Free Critic*. He has a PhD in Hebrew literature and writes weekly books reviews for *Yedioth Ahronoth*.

Irris Makler is a reporter and author based in Jerusalem. Her books include *Hope Street, Jerusalem* and *Our Woman in Kabul*.

Steven Nadler is Professor of Philosophy at the University of Wisconsin-Madison. His books include *Spinoza: A Life* and *Think Least of Death: Spinoza on How to Live and How to Die*.

Catherine Taylor is a writer, editor and critic, and the former deputy director of English PEN. Her memoir, *The Stirrings*, will be published in 2023.

Michael Vatikiotis has lived in South-East Asia for three decades, writing about politics and society. His latest book is *Lives Between the Lines: A Journey in Search of the Lost Levant*.

Amos Oz and A.B. Yehoshua
A tale of political twins

Nir Baram
(translated by Jessica Cohen)

"Come over again, we'll talk. There are decisive questions on the table: what sort of state are we going to have here?" said A.B. Yehoshua, at eighty-five, when we said goodbye at his apartment door exactly a month before his death.

I looked at him: he was gaunt and had trouble standing up, yet the familiar smile of curiosity and amusement was still on his face. It's impossible to understand what goes through the mind of someone approaching death, or to see the world as they see it. And in that moment, I understood even less. Why were these "decisive questions" preoccupying Yehoshua even as he acknowledged his impending death, talking of it openly and sometimes humorously? After all, we'd been debating these issues for seventeen years, and had never made the headway we'd hoped for. From where, even now, did he draw the strength, the curiosity, the concern for the future of this place? "I know how to fill life with hope," he once told me. Perhaps that was part of it.

Which "decisive questions" was Yehoshua referring to? Above all, there was one: the Israeli–Palestinian conflict and his new approach to solving it, on which he was very focused in his last years. Whenever we met, he expressed anger at my generation for not being sufficiently involved in political issues, for not making our voices heard. "If you take responsibility," he said, "you'll be more meaningful writers. You may not reach our status, which is unique and was created in the aftermath of the '67 war, but you will be meaningful." And he was absolutely right: Yehoshua and his literary peers had achieved an exceptional standing.

One topic that we only discussed openly at our last meeting was Yehoshua's relationship with Amos Oz, who had died in 2018. When I was a boy, in the 1980s, they were already considered the two most important Israeli writers.

"I had other friends," Yehoshua said, "but my friendship with Amos was the most significant. We used to show each other our manuscripts, and comment on them. That shows trust. I loved him, his sharpness and his integrity."

I asked if there was any competition between them.

"There was envy. Undoubtedly. I overcame the envy. I did not let it hurt our friendship. He gained more esteem and fame than I did, especially outside Israel. There aren't many writers I envied: all my envious energies were diverted to him. But I did not allow my envy to sabotage our friendship. And he envied me, too, because I was a more frequent object of literary research. I don't know if there's any such thing in your generation: a twin to deal with."

"We don't have that twin thing," I replied.

"That's not good – you must always have a twin: someone who annoys you but whom you love. Someone who pulls you ahead, and you him. And there's something else: the issue of responsibility. We felt responsible for Israel's political and moral image."

Yehoshua often spoke of responsibility and the author's role. To him, an author is not just a storyteller but a person with a moral role in society. Political involvement is practically an obligation, not a choice. Amos Oz and A.B. Yehoshua's standing in Israeli society was puzzling to many writers I met around the world, who saw themselves as storytellers, not moral voices. In fact, it was only after my own books were published in other languages and I met authors from different countries that I understood how uniquely Israeli was Yehoshua's and Oz's status. Of course there are politically active authors in other countries, but there are very few who can compete with the clout that both Oz and Yehoshua wielded.

These two authors did not create a new slot. The politically vocal author's position in Israel goes back to the circumstances of the state's founding, and to the importance attributed to intellectuals by political leaders – among them Israel's first prime minister, David Ben-Gurion – in a burgeoning society that needed both great stories and moral justifications. Most leaders of Mapai (the party that dominated Israel's political system in its first three decades and was the progenitor of the Labor Party) came from Eastern European cultures that gave considerable weight to writers' political stances.

Yehoshua correlates the status awarded to him and Oz in Israel (and beyond) to the Six-Day War of 1967

Political writers such as Yosef Haim Brenner were active in pre-state Israel, and the generation that preceded Yehoshua and Oz – known as "the 1948 Generation" – included several writers who were extremely political. The most prominent among them was Yizhar Smilansky (known as S. Yizhar), one of the greatest

Israeli writers, whose monumental *Days of Ziklag* probed the 1948 war, and who also wrote *Khirbet Khizeh*, a novella about the expulsion of Palestinians from a fictional village and the demolition of their homes, which provoked outrage when it came out. Yizhar was also a member of the Knesset. He was not an especially outspoken politician, devoting more time to writing than to legislation, but the fact that he was offered a seat in the Knesset by the ruling party indicates the importance of the politically involved writer in Israeli society.

It was not only in the centrist Mapai party but also on the Israeli right that intellectuals ran for parliament. "One could certainly say that in the young Israel, intellectuals held special status on the right, too," says Avi Shilon, who studies the Israeli right wing. "It's interesting that, unlike the centre-left, which focused more on prose writers, the right wing tended to embrace the Polish model of nationalism, which positioned poets alongside leaders as prophets of sorts. The poet Uri Zvi Greenberg served in this role, and was placed on the Herut party's list for the first Knesset by party leader Menachem Begin. Over the years, and with the decline in poetry's status in Israel, the alliance between poets and right-wing politicians subsided."

*

Yehoshua correlates the status awarded to him and Oz in Israel (and beyond) to the Six-Day War of 1967. To him, that was the turning point. After the war, many Israeli intellectuals were swept up by the country's widespread triumphalism. The "Greater Israel" movement, which advocated for settling the occupied territories, included former army generals and politicians, but also renowned intellectuals such as S.Y. Agnon (who had won the Nobel Prize in Literature a year earlier), author Haim Hazaz and poet Nathan Alterman. The occupation of the Western Wall in Jerusalem unleashed a yearning marked by messianic notes, which many secular Israelis found irresistible: the fulfilment of the Biblical vision of a "whole" Land of Israel. "The crux of this victory," wrote Alterman, "is that it erased the difference between the State of Israel and the Land of Israel. This is the first time since the destruction of the Second Temple that we possess the Land of Israel. State and land are now one."

A journalist who was affiliated with the Labor Party for many years and is avowedly secular once told me, only half-jokingly, that the Jewish claim to the land is based on the Biblical story of the covenant between the Jewish people and God: "In principle, we in the party believe that God gave us the land, but we wanted a secular state and so we decided He wasn't around anymore." One could argue that the Labor Party always used the Biblical narrative for its needs, which is why the post-1967 redemptive euphoria enthralled the party's secular wing, too.

> *Yehoshua believed that he did not have an underlying childhood wound like Oz did*

Agnon, Alterman and Hazaz, who all signed the petition for "Greater Israel", were not only a generation older than Oz (born in 1939) and Yehoshua (born in 1936), but also better known at the time. Although both the latter had grown up in Jerusalem, they had very different backgrounds. Yehoshua came from a longstanding Sephardi Jerusalemite family, and as a boy he accompanied his father to synagogue every Friday night. Oz grew up in a secular Ashkenazi family with ties to literary and academic circles. After his mother committed suicide when he was twelve, his family essentially fell apart, and he left Jerusalem as a teenager and moved to Kibbutz Hulda. "I was an 'outside kid' on the kibbutz, and I always wore the same clothes, the same underwear, the same socks. The kibbutz didn't pay for clothes for 'outside kids', and my father didn't pay either," he told his friend, the author Nurith Gertz. "I would go home to Jerusalem on the Sabbath and I had nothing, no one. I was completely isolated. Those were very bad years."

Oz and Yehoshua first met as teenagers, on those difficult weekends in Jerusalem. Oz recalls that he would come from the kibbutz and spend his time at the Scouts' meeting place, since he had no family to go home to. Yehoshua was a Scouts counsellor, and Oz remembered being one of his charges, but Yehoshua disputed that account and often told him: "You weren't there."

Yehoshua, unlike Oz, had a stable home life. "I was a good kid, and I gave a lot of support to my mother, who immigrated to Israel from Morocco and did not speak Hebrew," he told me. "My father loved me, even slightly admired me. I grew up appreciated and loved." Yehoshua believed that he did not have an underlying childhood wound like Oz did, and that he'd had a normal and fairly happy upbringing. Perhaps that is why he rarely wrote about his childhood and did not produce an autobiography, while Oz's greatest work, *A Tale of Love and Darkness*, is a memoir of his childhood in Jerusalem.

By 1967, Oz and Yehoshua were young men, gifted writers who had been publishing fiction and essays since the late 1950s. In 1965 Oz had published his first book, *Where the Jackals Howl*, a collection of short stories that drew popular attention and critical praise, while Yehoshua's acclaimed *Death of the Old Man*, from 1963, comprised short stories rich in imagination verging on the surreal, in a style very different to that of his predecessors, who mostly wrote social and psychological realism. Oz was better known than Yehoshua and more vocal in public, having been outspoken even before the war on controversial issues, including his support for former Minister of Defense Pinhas Lavon in his strident battle against Ben-Gurion. Both writers were perceived as principal members of Hebrew literature's future generation.

In August 1967, two months after the Six-Day War, Oz published a strongly worded editorial in *Davar*, the organ of the reigning Mapai party, in which he expressed unequivocal opposition to the writers and poets who supported the Greater Israel vision, and criticised those who had yet to weigh in on the question. Oz pointed to the profound moral failing of Israel's control over hundreds of thousands of Palestinians who were now without rights. In response to Moshe Dayan's assertion that "the Israeli administration does not depend on cooperation with the Arabs", Oz commented:

> These words are worrisome. Because they give off a whiff of the victor's intoxication, of arrogance and impatience. No government anywhere has lasted long without free cooperation on the part of its residents ... Even occupiers who took extreme steps in the path of oppression found themselves sitting on thorns and scorpions in most places – until they were removed. Not to mention the total moral devastation wrought by prolonged occupation on the occupier.

Oz's warning against this "moral devastation" marked the launch of his public political role. His positions set him apart from most well-known writers at the time, and also went against the Israeli zeitgeist. He had stripped the war of its exceptional mantle – the romantic, historic return of the Jews to their ancestral land – and likened the Israeli occupation to other occupations around the world.

A few months later, *The Seventh Day: Soldiers' Talk about the Six-Day War*, co-edited by Oz, presented the oral testimonies of kibbutz soldiers who had fought in the war. These young men talk about their experiences on the front, including accounts of looting and mistreating Arab prisoners of war. By relating ordinary soldiers' inner doubts, the book offered a very different picture than the familiar image of the victorious army. *The Seventh Day* provoked heated debate in Israel, with political leaders including Golda Meir viewing it as a vital document. Over the years, however, the book was also criticised for being a central part of the "shoot and weep" culture. Writing in *Haaretz*, in 2018, about the fiftieth-anniversary reissue, historian Tom Segev noted sardonically that the kibbutz ethos represented in the book "added to the self-image projected in the urban victory albums: not only mighty and heroic, but righteous, peace-loving, bleeding-heart boys. They are thoughtful, racked with doubt, sad, confused, tormented by the war." Segev believed the book was intended to protect the kibbutzniks' status among the Israeli elites.

At the end of 1967, some 250 intellectuals signed a public statement opposing the annexation of the newly occupied territories and the Greater Israel concept, and called on the state to "reinforce security and strive for peace as a supreme purpose of the state". Among the signatories were A.B. Yehoshua and Amos Oz. Yehoshua recognised that when it came to the war and its repercussions, Oz was ahead of both him and the majority of the intellectual elite at the time. In an opinion piece for *Yediot Aharonot* in 1982, he expressed his appreciation for Oz's prescience and courage: "It was Amos Oz who, immediately after the '67 war, before the sounds of gunfire had died down, launched a public political war. He was among the firmest, clearest, sharpest voices, and I believe also the most effective."

It is worth noting that the statement signed by the two writers in late 1967 was fairly moderate. It did not advocate a complete withdrawal from the territories, in contrast to the far-left socialist movement, Matzpen, which issued a much more strident manifesto at around the same time: "Holding on to the territories will turn us into a nation of murderers and murder victims. We must leave the occupied territories now!"

In 1967, my father, Uzi Baram, was a young leader in Mapai. Later in life he became a close friend of Oz's. I asked him what he thought of the positions taken by Oz and others at the time.

"The blatant way Oz spoke out against the government, and his warnings about moral collapse, seemed like hyperbole to us," he recalls. "We were all in a state of euphoria after the great victory. I wouldn't have signed the public statement that Oz and Yehoshua signed, because the idea of peace seemed impossible. But their rejection of the Greater Israel doctrine does reflect my own position in those years."

> *"Simply put? It was eventually proved that we were more prescient than the generation above us"*

"And what did you think of the Matzpen people, who called for an immediate withdrawal from the territories?"

"We thought they were crazy. Really crazy."

Oz and Yehoshua were not considered "crazy" by the Mapai leadership. Despite their critical stance, they were perceived as rooted in clear-cut Zionism. They were, to some extent, necessary voices. "The situation after '67," Yehoshua told me in that final meeting of ours, "was that the major writers didn't know what to do with the issue of the territories, and others were captivated by the mysticism of 'Greater Israel'. And then we turned up with a clear position. The war differentiated us from them, and that is where Amos and I began to sound a moral voice that became more and more acceptable. Many of the signatories to the Greater Israel petition later regretted their involvement. Simply put? It was eventually proved that we were more prescient than the generation above us."

*

On a Friday afternoon in mid-July 2022, hundreds of people crowd into a Tel Aviv auditorium to mark a month since Yehoshua's death. Among the participants are literary scholars, family members and actors who will read from plays based on Yehoshua's books. The president of Israel, Isaac Herzog, has sent a videotaped eulogy. It is not a surprise to see such a large crowd and so many emotional responses to Yehoshua's passing. As well as the loss of a beloved author, his death signifies the departure of the State Generation, of which he and Oz were the foremost representatives.

The event was organised by Avi Gil, who studies Yehoshua's life and work and was very close to him. He and I sit in a small room backstage and watch the crowds filing in. The overwhelming majority of attendees are from Yehoshua and Oz's generation, Israelis who started reading their work in the 1960s as young men and women, and who saw them as a political compass over the decades. They have come to say their farewells.

"Yehoshua had a very strong generational perception," says Gil, "and it was a significant component of his identity. He saw himself as part of a certain generation, and he wrote for that generation – his. That's why he often declared that he was ready to die, and in fact wanted to die. As he saw it, he was the last of the State Generation's prominent writers, and his time had come."

Gil and I discuss Yehoshua's "twin" concept, and his advice that I find my twin. As Yehoshua saw it, competitiveness, love and the whole complicated emotional turmoil that accompanies the notion of twins propelled him and Oz. I ask Gil about the ways in which Oz and Yehoshua were political twins.

"They met at a young age, studied at university together, sat in the same lectures, moved in the same literary milieu. As writers, they really did grow up together, and they also had common mentors, like Gershon Shaked, the influential scholar and critic. The affinity that evolved in those years would only become a friendship years later. Their perception of the '67 war and its outcomes was also similar: Oz was one step ahead, but Yehoshua did join him eventually. And after that, they acted in concert for many years."

"Did they believe they could influence public opinion?" I wonder.

"Far more than that: they had the profound sense that they were supposed to save Israel from the terrible consequences of the occupation, and promote the idea of peace."

"They actually wanted to *save* Israel?"

"Expressly so. That was their designation. They were both very Zionist, they believed that a state in which Jews were the majority was essential: this was a major convergence point between them. And they both believed that in order to preserve the Jewish democratic state, we must achieve peace. They were sceptical of politicians' commitment to human rights and peace, and felt that they had to constantly push the centre-left parties, in particular Labor, to end the occupation and resolve the conflict."

Until 1977, no one perceived Labor (Mapai's successor) as a left-wing party. It was a nationalistic, militaristic, centrist movement, far from willing to resolve the conflict and give up the West Bank or the Sinai and the Golan Heights, all of which had been occupied in the 1967 war. Oz certainly shared this opinion of the party, and before the 1977 elections he came out publicly against voting for Labor, which was then led by Shimon Peres. After the dramatic reversal in the 1977 elections, when Likud took power, Labor remained a long way from the peace plan that would become its hallmark fifteen years later. Yisrael Galili, a senior Labor politician, outlined the party's post-election position: "It is most essential that, even as an opposition movement, we not fall into a negative polarisation in terms of the continued settlement effort, the opposition to the establishment of a Palestinian state, and the opposition to a return to the June 1967 borders."

My father, who was on the left end of the Labor spectrum, believes that Oz and Yehoshua's true influence crystalised in the late 1970s and into the 1980s, when the notion of the occupation as a cancer in the body of the Jewish state gained traction, and there was a constant prodding of Labor voters towards the idea of peace. Many factors contributed to this shift, including the emergence of Peace Now as a large protest movement, and pivotal events such as the Lebanon War and the First Intifada. But in his opinion, Oz and Yehoshua's role in Labor's newfound emphasis on Israeli–Palestinian reconciliation should not be underestimated.

"A man like Yisrael Galili couldn't have imagined that the peace party of the '90s was the same party he'd belonged to for decades, and that change resulted, in part, from Oz and Yehoshua's consistent work," my father says. A similar argument can be heard on the right: Amnon Lord, a journalist and right-wing activist, wrote that "Oz and Yehoshua moved the Labor Party far to the left".

My father and others also point out Oz's direct influence on Shimon Peres when it came to the Palestinian issue. Their well-known friendship lasted for many years, and both men boasted of it at various points. In the 1970s, Peres was considered further to the right than Rabin, and actively supported the construction of settlements. Yet in the 1990s he became the figure most identified with the peace effort.

The audience is sitting down now, and I feel a slight tremble. I'm supposed to speak about Yehoshua's attitude towards young writers, and about my relationship with him over the years. I feel overwhelmed by all the stories I can tell. I first met Yehoshua when I went to his home in Haifa to interview him for *Haaretz*, and we remained friends ever since. I remember his repeated demand that I should become a father. He once said that he knew fatherhood would give me more stability and help me personally, and he declared that he wouldn't read any more of my books until I had a child. It was a sort of regular joke we shared, but it says a lot about the way he viewed his friends: never as a means to an end, but as full, complex human beings.

> *"Amos once advised him to delve deeper into his characters' psychology, but Yehoshua was interested in investigating ideas and moral quandaries"*

I ask Gil about Yehoshua and Oz as literary twins.

"Yehoshua felt that they were twins in the first few decades, but starting in the '80s, when he began publishing his great novels – *The Lover*, *Mr. Mani* – he viewed them as quite far apart, stylistically. Amos once advised him to delve deeper into his characters' psychology, as he did in a number of his own books, but Yehoshua was interested in investigating ideas and moral quandaries in his writing. So he believed that as writers they had grown apart, but still perceived them as political twins."

Oz also spoke of "the moral issue" as something that differentiated his and Yehoshua's writing, and he was far less enthusiastic about fiction that engages with moral questions. In *What Makes an Apple?* he explains: "I have an ongoing argument about this with A.B. Yehoshua, who locates the issue of morality at the forefront of literary creation ... I think there is a moral dimension in a different sense: putting yourself for a few hours under another person's skin, or in another person's shoes. It has an indirect moral weight, although it's not very heavy, let's not exaggerate."

As we walk to the auditorium, we come across two older women paging through Yehoshua's *The Lover*. "Let's go, it's starting soon," an older man urges them. One of the women looks at him and says, "On the contrary: it's already over."

*

Beyond their different approaches to writing, Oz and Yehoshua had distinct attitudes about their ability to leverage their influence. Oz met regularly with Israeli politicians, travelled to international meetings and was acquainted with leaders around the world. Yehoshua, conversely, did not maintain close ties with politicians. (One exception was former president Reuven Rivlin, a friend from their days in the Scouts youth movement in Jerusalem.)

Yehoshua recalled that Oz used to phone him and report on his discussions with political leaders. At times, Yehoshua believed that Oz had too much faith in these meetings. Yehoshua did not hold contemporary politicians in high esteem, nor did he usually believe them. Politicians, for their part, strove to maintain ties with both Oz and Yehoshua – sometimes for prestige and sometimes out of curiosity. Mostly these were members of left-wing parties, such as Peres, Ehud Barak and others. Inviting a writer or intellectual to one's home for counsel has been a familiar ritual for Israeli politicians ever since the state's founding days, and from the late 1970s onwards, Oz and Yehoshua were two of the most prominent intellectuals in the country. Despite differing on the utility of ties with politicians, the two writers shared a clear goal: resolving the Israeli–Palestinian conflict. Oz believed – and when it came to Peres, he might have been right – that direct influence on leaders was an important means of effecting change.

Meanwhile, in the public arena, they collaborated frequently: signing petitions, speaking at protest rallies and conferences, supporting political leaders. They called for a national unity government after the 1984 elections, and expressed vocal opposition to the wars in Lebanon – the first (in 1982), and the second (together with David Grossman, whose son was killed at the very end of that war, in 2006). They also acted independently, as with Oz's appeal ahead of the 1977 elections. Of course, they also wrote about issues other than the Israeli–Palestinian conflict: secularism, ethnic tensions, Israeliness versus Jewishness, identity questions and so forth – but most of their energy was devoted to the peace process.

They did have disagreements – for example, regarding Israel's national character. In the 1980s, Yehoshua came to believe that Israel must integrate within the Mediterranean sphere, at least culturally, and forge an identity that would not be wholly alien in the Middle East. "Yehoshua is completely serious when he asks whether it is possible to switch identities or travel on a 'cross-identity' path," wrote Dan Miron, considered the greatest State

Generation literary critic. "Identity is necessary," he continues, "but the ability to transcend it and break through its borders is no less necessary."

Oz was unconvinced by the idea of integration, fearing it would have a negative impact on Israel's political and legal systems, and on Israeli democracy, which he thought should embrace the Western model. These differences likely stemmed in part from the two men's different backgrounds: Yehoshua's father, who spoke Arabic, was very familiar with the neighbouring cultures, while Oz observed Arab culture from a distance, like most political leaders of the time – people with a distinctly European orientation. These disagreements, however, seemed minor at the end of the twentieth century, a time when both acknowledged that integrating within the Middle East was not practical until the most urgent matter had been resolved: the Israeli–Palestinian conflict.

"We had a lot of disagreements around the priorities of the Israeli left," says the writer and historian Fania Oz-Salzberger, Amos Oz's daughter. "While I held that gender equality and social justice were no less vital than liberating the Palestinian people, Dad and Yehoshua both gave top priority to the occupation, which demanded certain alliances (for example with the ultra-Orthodox) that would delay any progress on issues such as gender equality. To their mind, it was a price worth paying." Furthermore, Oz-Salzberger detects something very masculine in their position: "They always said: the first thing is the occupation, the Israeli–Palestinian issue. After that, we'll address the other issues. On social-economic matters, for example, they were both fairly superficial socialists, and did not devote a lot of thought to those matters."

*

In 2011, there was keen public debate in Israel around a potential attack against Iran. Haim Oron, at the time a member of Knesset with Meretz and a close friend of Oz's, was a sort of liaison between two groups: the first comprised military men, like the former chief of staff Amnon Lipkin-Shahak and former Mossad chair Meir Dagan, and the second included intellectuals, led by Oz, with Yehoshua among them. The two groups united around a common goal: stop the planned Israeli attack on Iran, or at least delay it as long as possible. Oron recalls that Oz was acting on behalf of Peres, who by then was president of Israel, a largely symbolic role that precluded him from expressing his position publicly, and that Oz's involvement in the group's activity was daily.

Oz wrote an appeal that both groups were to sign, which asserted that it was not Israel's job to finish the anti-Iran campaign: it should be left to the United States. The fact that former generals (considered a public authority on Iran) and intellectuals (who were not perceived as strategic experts on the Iran nuclear question) were able to join forces says a lot about the latter group's standing in certain circles of Israeli society.

> *"Perhaps Eli Yishai viewed Amos as the rabbi of centre-left secular Israelis"*

"I saw Amos's involvement in the Iranian question as a natural step," says Oron. "I'm a member of Amos's generation, and in leftist circles we always valued intellectuals' opinions. Here's an example: in the early '70s, a few officers had reservations about the army's belligerent conduct in Gaza, so we held an event in Tel Aviv to discuss the issue. Imagine this: Prime Minister Golda Meir attended. Amos was one of the speakers, and he asked Golda, 'What do you dream about at night?' She answered, 'I don't have time to dream. I can't sleep because the phone rings at night with updates on casualties.' Why had Amos been invited? Because his participation gave the event a certain depth, a broader context."

I ask Oron: "For politicians, was it mainly ostentation, and tradition? Or is there a real benefit to encounters between politicians and intellectuals?"

"I often sought advice from Amos, but also from Yehoshua, on political questions: from the future of the state to whether I should run for the Meretz leadership. To me, Oz had a rare ability to put things into words, a capacity to distil the essence of whatever was being discussed. Many politicians publicly used phrases they'd heard from Oz in private conversations. But forget about me for a moment – it made sense for *me* to talk with Amos. The question is why right-wing politicians wanted ties with him."

"And what is the answer?"

"It's not like politicians on the right had anything to gain politically from being associated with Amos. But look: Eli Yishai, when he was the leader of the Sephardi religious party, Shas, wanted me to introduce him to Oz, even though his constituents had no sympathy for Oz. I set up a meeting for them at my home. Yishai saw Amos as a sort of gateway to secular Israelis, and perhaps also an authority in that sector. Rabbi Ovadia Yosef was the supreme authority in Shas, and perhaps Yishai viewed Amos as a parallel figure: the rabbi of centre-left secular Israelis."

"What happened when they met?"

"They sat together for long, deep talks, which veered from the future of the conflict, to questions about the degree of secularism in the country to tensions between Sephardim and Ashkenazim. Naftali Bennett also met with Amos a few times. I find it interesting that young right-wingers from a completely different generation saw Oz as an authority."

Oz understood his unique status in Israeli society, and he was also aware of the resentment and envy it aroused. "He was everywhere and nowhere," he said of himself in *What Makes an Apple?*, "even prime ministers ask to meet with him, and he gets quoted on the radio, in the newspapers. There's almost no leftist movement he isn't in some way centrally involved in. He's at all the big protest rallies in Malchei Israel Square ... The Israeli arena is small, hardly touched by a single ray of sun, so why does that ray always shine on him? He should step aside."

*

While Oz was identified for many years with Meretz, Yehoshua was more of a "free agent" in his political commitment, and at times supported Labor (in the 2006 elections, for example). In fact, some veteran members of the Labor Party remember Yehoshua, more than Oz, as having frequently attended party meetings. One recalls: "Yehoshua was a fiery orator, full of passion and pathos, who appeared before us as a prophet of apocalypse, reprimanding us for ignoring the occupation and for the wrongs we were inflicting on our children. I saw Oz give speeches at the big Peace Now rallies, and he was a wonderfully articulate speaker, choosing every word carefully. But I remember Yehoshua's speeches more clearly: the fervour, the way he would suddenly upset the audience with an unexpected statement. As an orator, it was like he came from a different place."

That "different place" manifested not only in his reproachful speeches but in his flexibility of thought. He was a man with huge curiosity, unafraid of new ideas, who relished the opportunity to engage with beliefs opposed to his own. Menachem Peri, Yehoshua's editor, contrasts the writer's political stances, where he advanced "sane ideas, in support of national normalcy", with his books, in which "there is an anarchic element. His literature undermines the considered notions in his essays and throws chaos into the world order, thereby celebrating the vitality of abandoned freedom."

I propose a slightly different read to Peri: could it be that the difference he sees between Yehoshua's fiction and his political notions is not that clear-cut, and that the freedom Yehoshua allowed in his fiction bled into his politics? As, for example, in his contention that a Jew who does not live in Israel is a "partial Jew" (a notion that many people found outrageous, and which aroused fury both in Israel and abroad). Or in his concept of merging identities to create a Middle Eastern Arab-Jew, which among the Zionist left was viewed as a preposterous fantasy.

"There is something to that," Peri replies after some thought. "He did have a measure of irony towards political ideas in general. In his novels, every solution is doomed to fail. Characters who believe in solutions are often put in provocative situations, like Luria from *The Tunnel*, a man in a state of dementia, barely functional, who delivers knowledgeable lectures on how to resolve the conflict. And I recall something else: we once appeared at a campaign event for Peres, and Yehoshua got on stage and threw a bomb: he said that nations come together through civil war, and that he had concluded there was no choice but to wage a civil war in Israel. The crowd was stunned, and Peres was horrified – he was afraid Yehoshua's declaration would doom his election chances."

Peri says that he and Yehoshua liked to play around with outlandish ideas and invent apocalyptic scenarios. For example, they would imagine that after their deaths the Jewish state ceased to exist, and debate where their grandchildren would live, who would rule the country and what would become of Israeli literature. Yehoshua's enthusiasm for new ideas went beyond his talks with Peri: his distance from politicians allowed him to throw brash ideas into the public space, ones that might have seemed impractical but that had the power to expand political thought in Israel. In his novel *A Late Divorce*, which expresses profound pessimism regarding "an end to the conflict", Yehoshua implies that the conflict injects energy and vitality, both into Israelis and into Palestinians, and that separating the two nations would spell a death of sorts. As Peri wrote, "The conflict relationship is a crazy one, full of vigor that one cannot keep living in but cannot get out of."

Yehoshua admitted that he wanted to be liked, but he was not afraid to anger people and did not shy away from harsh disagreements – he even enjoyed them. He often said things that invited the ire of both left and right circles, yet his public persona never provoked the starkly emotional opposition that Oz attracted. Yigal Schwartz, a professor of literature, once wrote that Oz aroused such extreme responses in the cultural arena that it was hard to decipher their logic or roots. On one hand there were displays of love and admiration, and on the other hand disgust and hatred.

Of course, there are many reasons for the different public treatment of the two writers, including their backgrounds (Oz, unlike Yehoshua, was perceived as a member of the Ashkenazi elite), their public personas and their speaking styles. But there was another

> *"Yehoshua's wild and imaginative side was not fulfilled in his personal life"*

significant difference, which Avi Gil underscores: "Oz's life was more public, while Yehoshua ultimately led a very quiet life. His focus was on his home and family: he wrote every morning, went to the university to teach, and came back home." Peri adds, simply: "Yehoshua lived the grey life of a bureaucrat. His wild and imaginative side was not fulfilled in his personal life, because he was afraid to let it. That side emerged mainly in his books, and perhaps also in his ideas."

*

Most acquaintances of Oz and Yehoshua point to the 1980s as the period in which their friendship was cemented. They were, in fact, part of a triangle that included their peer and fellow writer Yehoshua Kenaz. Unlike Oz and Yehoshua, Kenaz enjoyed almost unanimous critical acclaim (with rare exceptions). Although he also signed petitions and occasionally collaborated with Oz and Yehoshua on political actions, he rarely spoke in public and was not seen as a political figure. The three men met regularly to have dinner and discuss books, writers and life in general. Of course, they also talked politics.

"They exchanged honest, probing comments on each other's manuscripts. They had a genuine literary dialogue," Peri says. "They were not a literary group or a movement, they each had a distinct concept of literature, and of course there was also jealousy, but they did build a friendship and a mutual trust that certainly strengthened them."

While Yehoshua confessed to some professional envy of Oz, it seems that Oz developed his own envy, rooted in a completely different facet. "Dad viewed Yehoshua as a whole person, full of self-confidence, who had grown up in a loving, supportive family that was the polar opposite of his own," says Oz-Salzberger. "He saw in Yehoshua a sociable man who felt completely at ease in the company of others, with an unshakeable belief in himself and his capabilities."

"Wasn't Amos self-confident?" I ask her. "After all, when you heard how eloquently and sharply he spoke, you would never have imagined that this was a man who harboured self-doubts."

"Dad grew up with no self-confidence. With a profound sense of unworthiness. People often said his family had been privileged, partly because of his uncle, Yosef Klausner, a highly respected historian and literary scholar. But that connection only intensified Amos's feelings of inferiority. His father was an unfulfilled, downtrodden man, and when the family got together Amos saw how small his father was compared to Klausner. His mother, who was clinically depressed and probably also psychotic, committed suicide, and everything fell apart completely."

I tell Oz-Salzberger about a meeting I had with Amos at his home in 2016. I had just returned from a year-long journey around the West Bank, full of doubts about the feasibility of dividing the country, and had published an account of my travels in *A Land Without Borders*. Oz explained to me that I'd lost hope too soon, that the two-state solution was the only possible one, and he showered me with examples of historical changes that no one had predicted. While I was full of questions and despair, I sensed that the man in front of me was an optimist, who knew with absolute certainty where the country should be heading. He almost managed to convince me that precisely because I was looking at the conflict from up close, I'd lost sight of the right answers.

"You have to understand," Oz-Salzberger says, "Dad had a need to charm people, to fascinate them, to bewitch them – in order to earn his keep, to feel worthy. He didn't simply host people – he wasn't just hosting you when you visited him at home. He always had to deliver the goods, to impress his guests with a wonderful show of eloquence. Otherwise he felt like he was nothing."

I tell Oz-Salzberger that I can understand that personality trait. I admit that I wouldn't have associated it with her father, but I do understand the feeling that you can never relax and just *be*.

"Yes, that was Dad. But Yehoshua, the way Dad saw it, was self-assured, very successful, with a positive view of himself, a joie de vivre and a love of sensuous pleasures. Of course, Dad knew how complex Yehoshua was, but ultimately he envied him for the way he experienced life. Notice how in most of Yehoshua's books there are more sensuous pleasures than in Dad's, and also that the men in Yehoshua's books are usually more stable, quite happily married, or at least they used to be, and they usually have money. Dad's protagonists are unhappy, disconnected, aimless."

"Then how do you explain the fact that Amos roared into the public arena at an early age, with great confidence in his opinions and a desire to explain to prime ministers how wrong they were? Considering the personality you depict, he should have had fears and doubts – that he would be hated, that he would be exposed."

"I'll put it simply," she replies. "Politics was the place where he demonstrated his masculinity, his machismo. He was not an assertive man in the personal sphere, but when it came to politics, he was able to externalise a strong, all-knowing manliness. When he was young, he envied the commando unit officers and the combatants on the kibbutz, and in the political world he conducted himself like an alpha male, like a leader. Apart from the ideological issues, that was another reason he liked his political work. He created an assertive political persona that gave him strength."

An interesting fact about Oz concerns his involvement in the legendary, longstanding hostilities between Shimon Peres and Yitzhak Rabin. After Rabin published his 1979 memoir, in which he attacked Peres, Oz would go back and forth between the two politicians' homes in the same northern Tel Aviv neighbourhood to try to help them reconcile. Many other people also mediated between Rabin and Peres over the decades, but that does not make it any less difficult to picture one of Israel's greatest writers shuttling between the apartments of these political adversaries.

Oz's political involvement had a decisively practical bent, and he was willing to do the legwork. He was also exposed to sensitive information. He was one of very few people in Israel who knew about the Oslo talks – and was familiar with details of the negotiations – long before government ministers learned about the secret channel. In this respect, the difference between Oz and Yehoshua is deeper than it might seem, and perhaps calls into question the "political twin" notion. Oz was more enmeshed in the political world than any other Israeli writer.

> *Oz used to claim that we in Israel followed the intelligentsia model, in which writers find a listening ear in the halls of government*

The way Oz worked politically was moulded by something the philosopher Isaiah Berlin once told him. He said that intellectuals are a Western phenomenon, and that there is always something detached about them: they are removed from the beating pulse of life. Whereas the intelligentsia is an Eastern European invention that could have an enormous impact. Oz used to claim that we in Israel followed the intelligentsia model, in which writers find a listening ear in the halls of government. He felt that this held true until the rule of Benjamin Netanyahu, who cut off the communication between representatives of the intelligentsia and the regime. Netanyahu was the first prime minister who did not meet with Oz or Yehoshua. To him, they were part of the hostile leftist elites and were not to be ascribed any moral superiority.

*

In the 2000s, after the failure of the Israeli left's peace project, the two main leftist parties, Labor and Meretz (which in 1992 had jointly held almost half the seats in the Knesset), were gradually reduced to marginal parties that represented roughly 10 per cent of the electorate. Oz and Yehoshua were no longer leading voices in a large political camp with aspirations to rule the country and a desire to effect changes, but part of a weakened, powerless sector.

"Writers like Oz, Yehoshua and others used to publish a book and it was like a leader speaking to his constituents, saying this is how one must write: this is literature!" says Peri. "And writers also believed in their duty to lead political thought. That world is gone. Now what writers have, at most, is some new book and some political opinion. Oz and Yehoshua both understood that."

Fania Oz-Salzberger adds: "The last time Dad felt he was influential was during the Second Lebanon War, in 2006, when they called for an end to the war. In the Netanyahu years, he felt he had no real influence."

The two writers' recognition that their influence had waned and that the Israeli–Palestinian conflict had vanished from the public agenda was the background to the most significant political rift between them.

In the middle of the last decade, Yehoshua, whose proclivity for audacious ideas I have mentioned, decided to abandon the two-state solution. He reached this position after serious deliberation, but once he had, he did so publicly and directly. "For fifty years I supported the two-state solution, but to my regret it is now impossible," he announced in an interview for the Israeli news website *Walla*. "We cannot remove 400,000 Jews from the West Bank. It's over." Yehoshua concluded that Jews and Palestinians were too enmeshed and could no longer be separated. "I did not want the territories, but we're stuck with them," he said. He also attacked supporters of the two-state solution, who he thought were clinging to a dream that could not be realised. In my talks with him, he called them "detached".

Yehoshua's move was presented, including by himself, as an attainment of sobriety, and he began talking about the urgent need to present new ideas. He eventually laid out his new vision for resolving the conflict in a series of essays in *Haaretz* and in several interviews. As he saw it, we were already living in a one-state reality, and the question now was simple: would it be a democracy or an apartheid state? Yehoshua, naturally favouring the former, suggested naturalising the Palestinians (who currently lack rights) as citizens of the state.

As a man who was embedded in the Zionist left for decades, Yehoshua understood Israelis' fear that such a state would ultimately have an Arab majority, and he tried to mollify their anxieties through the concept of containment. "Israel will absorb the Palestinians within it," he proposed, meaning that the Palestinians would undergo a sort of "Israelisation" process, "the way we did with the Palestinian Israelis, whose integration is a success story by any measure."

The containment idea enabled Yehoshua to argue that in this single state there would be no bitter competition between Jews and

Palestinians over control. Instead, he believed, a shared identity would gradually evolve, which would be predominantly Israeli but feature certain Arab characteristics. Yehoshua essentially positioned himself midway between the one-state camp – which advocates citizenship for all, with no collective identity – and the two-state camp. He recognised that the process would be long, complicated and difficult, and he knew it would be next to impossible to find Palestinian partners for a deal that demanded they give up aspects of their national identity and become more Israeli.

Yehoshua spoke of the new idea with hopefulness, but Menachem Peri saw his despair: "In our conversations, perhaps in part under my influence, he expressed extreme pessimism about the future and about finding a solution to the conflict. In my opinion, his whole concept of the one-state solution stemmed from despair. He felt that it was all over, that even the left no longer took an interest in the Palestinians, so he clutched at this vision."

I always saw in Yehoshua a man with a rare talent for hopefulness, and so his decision to promote a particular model of the single state did not come as a shock to me. Peri's claim that the new vision resulted in part from despair is probably correct, and brings to mind our own conversations, which veered from excitement about the idea to a despondent recognition that "there is no chance for peace" – sometimes within the same sentence. Ultimately, Yehoshua knew that a significant portion of the Israeli left accepted his basic premise that the two-state solution had become moot, and had therefore given up hope. Yehoshua came to acknowledge that it was no longer possible to divide the land, but he would not abandon his yearning for peace: he felt it was his responsibility to sketch a horizon of hope.

"If previously Yehoshua had strived for a clearly defined Jewish-Israeli identity in a Jewish state, now he was saying to himself: maybe we won't be so well defined, we'll become more blurred, we'll mingle with one another a little," explains Avi Gil. "For years he spoke of a certain integration in the Middle East but within the parameters of a Jewish state. Now he was taking a big leap forward."

Oz did not like Yehoshua's new idea at all. He'd always seen a Jewish democratic state as vital: a home for a nation that had learned from history how desperately it needed its own place. To him, Yehoshua's solution not only endangered the Jewish state but undermined the only hope for peace. "Dad was saddened to his last day that Yehoshua had despaired of the two-state solution, which they had championed together," says Oz-Salzberger. "Dad claimed there was no other way. He always said: 'I completely support a world in which there are no more nation-states and we all live in one loving community, but what I'm saying is this: we can't be the first to dismantle the nation-state.'"

The two authors had profound talks around Yehoshua's change of heart. Haim Oron, who was invited to some of their conversations, recounts that "in those discussions, Amos was insistent that giving up on the two-state solution was irresponsible and dangerous. They mostly maintained a friendly tone, but the disagreement was palpable, as was Amos's disappointment. Every so often he would take a jab at Yehoshua, saying something like, 'So, you're still hawking that idea?' Yehoshua stood his ground, saying there was no other choice, and that in order to save Israeli democracy we had to change course."

"Even when they visited their friend Yehoshua Kenaz together, when he was very ill," Avi Gil adds, "they conducted turbulent debates at his bedside. To the best of my knowledge, A.B. Yehoshua did not know at the time that Amos himself was very ill."

Even after they'd said goodbye to each other, the debate seemed to continue. "Every so often Dad would throw out something about how Yehoshua had let his imagination transport him to a very unrealistic and half-baked solution to the Israeli–Palestinian conflict," says Oz-Salzberger. Friends of Yehoshua recall that he realised that he'd angered not only Oz, but most of the Zionist-left political milieu, to which he'd belonged for decades. Oz's opposition, however, seemed to preoccupy him especially. In one of our conversations, Yehoshua told me that he still hoped Oz would come around to new ideas or at least acknowledge that the two-state era was over, but deep inside he knew the chances were slim. In a similar vein, Oz slowly understood that Yehoshua's new idea was not some passing whim, but that his political twin – or former twin – had moved into a distant realm.

Oz himself did not stand still, politically, in his final years. "I had many conversations with Oz in the last years of his life," my father says. "I think he changed some of the positions that had moulded him in the '60s, particularly regarding Ben-Gurion. He was a strident opponent of Ben-Gurion when he was young, but now he started applauding him for having saved democracy by appointing liberal judges to the first Supreme Court, and in general he began speaking of Ben-Gurion as the most important leader, worthy of extraordinary esteem."

Regarding Yehoshua's change, my father says, Oz was unambiguous: "Oz was amazed at the change Yehoshua had gone through. He believed Yehoshua was wrong and was influenced by radical leftists. He was certainly angry at him, too, and felt he was weakening the entire camp. And there was something else: Oz felt that on political issues he himself had always been the ringleader, the chief instigator, whom Yehoshua had joined. But now all of a sudden Yehoshua was kicking their main concept to the curb."

"Sometimes I would meet Yehoshua on a Sunday," says Peri, "and he'd tell me, 'I met Oz this weekend and we had a difficult talk.' It was clear that the political rift was not easy for him. I would tell him, 'Don't you think you're both wasting your energy? After all, at the moment no one is talking about your idea or Amos's. It's all completely hypothetical.'"

Indeed, many people might find the two men's lively debates puzzling. Beginning in 2000, with the Second Intifada, talks of peace evaporated from public discourse in Israel, and in the Netanyahu years there was no more mention of resolving the conflict. Even the left, which attacked Netanyahu around the clock, hardly criticised him for the absence of a peace plan. Yet despite there being no hope on the horizon for renewed negotiations, and with the conflict now perceived even among the left as a non-starter, still these two writers sat around debating the finer points of the resolution to the conflict.

> *"Even when I visited Amos at hospital, we kept arguing"*

They were aware of the disconnect between their own conversations and Israeli reality, but they seem to have felt that some of their responsibility, some of the political role they had filled for so many years, was to not abandon the attempt to propose a way out of the conflict, even if they themselves doubted its feasibility.

"Even when I visited Amos at hospital, we kept arguing," Yehoshua told me sadly, "but when I realised how ill he was, I decided to drop it, not to anger him even more. I told him, 'Amos, let's leave it for now. First get better, and then we'll discuss everything.'"

*

The last years of the two men's lives accentuated their different approaches to politics. While Yehoshua was enthusiastically promoting his new vision, which many of his friends found bold and which was, by his own admission, aimed at the distant future, Oz, despite his illness, was focused on completely pragmatic political issues. He was involved in efforts to remove Netanyahu, although he understood that these endeavours (most of which came from the political centre) did not offer hope for change on the Israeli–Palestinian front. He remained a supporter of Meretz, but now devoted time to a practical political initiative that did not dwell on theoretical concepts but on governance.

"Oz met with [Benny] Gantz, [Gabi] Ashkenazi, Ehud Barak and others, and was very active in the attempt to establish a broad front, a sort of security-focused centrist party, which would unseat Netanyahu," says my father. "He was close to Gantz and to others. And it should be noted: they initiated the meetings with him – he was the person whose approval they sought."

In the long run-up to the April 2019 elections, a number of generals wanted to run together (Gabi Ashkenazi, Ehud Barak, Moshe Ya'alon and Benny Gantz) but they disagreed on who would head the future party. "Oz was involved in resolving the question of leadership," says my father. "He consulted with me on how to create a mechanism – for example, public opinion polls – which would allow them to decide who would lead the party without prompting the others to drop out."

Amos Oz passed away in December 2018. In January 2019, Blue and White – the centrist alliance aiming to replace Netanyahu – was announced. It's true that the political dispute between Oz and Yehoshua had not been resolved before his death, and that Yehoshua continued to promote his new vision up until his death in

June 2022, but it seems that their years of collaboration at the end of the last century (when their public impact was at its high point) left a deeper impression on Israeli society than their disagreement.

"He was a brave man and a wonderful writer, a man who fulfilled himself," said Yehoshua about Oz after he died. Similar things can be said of Yehoshua. It's reasonable to assume that the process of saying goodbye to these two authors, who had been a visible presence in Israeli society for decades, is far from over, and that the void they left will not be filled. Even in their final years, both were extremely accomplished writers, but their political status and their perception of the author's role had evolved in a different time, a distant era that my generation experienced as children, and which our children will only read about.

After the prophets
The next generation of Israeli writers

Arik Glasner
(translated by Jessica Cohen)

In December 2018, the author Amos Oz died at the age of seventy-nine. Two years later, Yehoshua Kenaz died (of Covid-19) at eighty-three. And two years after that, in June 2022, A.B. Yehoshua died at eighty-five. And so, within the space of four years, three of the foremost Hebrew writers of any generation – who were also all good friends – were lost. (Kenaz, though the least known of the three internationally, is considered by many in the Israeli literary community – myself included – to have been, at his peak, and especially in his novel *Infiltration*, the most accomplished.)

Yehoshua, Oz and Kenaz represent the generation of writers born around the 1930s, which was, in hindsight, second only to the "Revival Generation": those born in the 1870s and 1880s, whose number included, among many others, Yosef Haim Brenner, S.Y. Agnon and the poet H.N. Bialik. Other prominent members of this later generation include Yaakov Shabtai, the foremost, thanks to his novels *Past Continuous* (1977) and *Past Perfect* (1984), as well as Aharon Appelfeld, Amalia Kahana-Carmon, Yitzhak Ben Ner and Dan Tsalka; poets Nathan Zach and Dahlia Ravikovitch; and playwright Hanoch Levin.

This talented cohort was dubbed the "State Generation", having launched their literary careers after the State of Israel was established and had become an irrefutable fact. Their dominance has not yet abated, its members defeated only by biology – not sociology. New generations of writers have emerged, charting, decade by decade, their nation's distinctive political and social turns. Although in many respects the generation personified by these three impressive forebears has not been supplanted, more recent literary movements have explored other imaginative territories and are worthy of attention in their own right.

*

First, however, we must ask *why* the State Generation was so remarkable. Was it a fluke, or can we identify the causes?

The answers to such questions are usually complex, yet they can be surprisingly straightforward. I've always found it astonishing that one little Russian town of roughly 10,000 residents (about a third of whom were Jewish) was home, in the latter part of the nineteenth century, to two of the greatest Hebrew writers, Yosef Haim Brenner (1881–1921) and Uri Nissan Gnessin (1879–1913), who met at the local yeshiva and became good friends. What were the odds, I wondered, that these two prodigies' paths would intersect? I finally realised that the answer was in the question: there is nothing to nurture a great talent quite like the close proximity of another great talent. And so it is certainly possible that the dynamics of mutual competition (which arose once a few of its members began to stand out) led the State Generation to such impressive feats.

A.B. Yehoshua, however, proposed a different way to understand the uniqueness of his generation. In a 1998 collection of essays, *Achizat Moledet* ("The Grasp of Homeland"), he wrote:

> What made this generation so dominant in Hebrew literature, not only in a purely literary sense but also in terms of its rich interaction with its readership? I think that, from the first, we had an interesting balance between the hidden and the revealed. What I mean is that there were secret compartments within us, hidden drawers that were gradually opened through our years of artistic creation.

And these "hidden drawers", he explains, are usually autobiographical. For Yehoshua, it was his Sephardi roots, which began peeking through the "normative" Israeli façade. For Amos Oz, it was his mother's suicide and his upbringing in a Revisionist family. For Appelfeld, it was the pre-war Jewish world. All these were "powerful elements that were initially hidden, out of a desire to be more congruent with Israeli society's core values".

I believe these "hidden drawers" (to which we may add gender-based and sexual nonconformity, as well as the profoundly nihilistic urges displayed by some writers of the generation, all of which contributed to the complexity of their writing) may be seen as a conflict between the "Israeli normalcy" presented by the newly founded state and the extant "Jewishness", which was convoluted and neurotic. In other words: this generation emerged after the great battle over the establishment of the state, once the road had (ostensibly) been paved to a new, ordinary, simple life, borne on the wings of a young, optimistic Israeli identity. Within this reality, "abnormal" elements began to simmer – elements that were pessimistic, anomalous, painful, elderly, "Jewish" and unassimilated.

We then begin to see similarities between the State Generation and the earlier Revival Generation. There, too, there was a fruitful tension between the young, enthusiastic, future-facing Zionist-Hebrew identity and the old, diasporic, obstructive Jewish world. Both generations operated under similar pressures and within a productive tension between "old" and "new", leading to great literary triumphs.

After the prophets

The subsequent literary generation, comprising those born in the 1950s, was not perceived as challenging its predecessors. Rather, superb writers such as David Grossman (born in 1954), Zeruya Shalev (born in 1959) and Youval Shimoni (born in 1955) view themselves as following in their forerunners' footsteps.

The State Generation's reign over Hebrew literature was not threatened until the 1990s, which in many parts of the world seemed like a glittering new post–Cold War era. In Israel it appeared no less promising, because of the hopes offered by the Oslo Accords and their vision of a "new Middle East", and due to a sense of prosperity and vibrant consumerism generated by the transition to a neoliberal economy. In this carefree, post-ideological decade, Hebrew literature (much like world literature) saw a blossoming of postmodernism, one of whose features is a scepticism towards the sanctity of the artistic act, and towards seriousness itself. (Andy Warhol is, to my mind, the central formulator of the postmodern *Weltanschauung*.)

Two brilliant representatives of Israeli postmodernism are Orly Castel-Bloom (born in 1960) and Etgar Keret (born in 1967), who took the literary world by storm and offered a completely new approach to the figure of the author. First, they demonstratively rebuffed the mantle of "prophet" or "public intellectual" that Oz and Yehoshua had worn. Second, they adopted a crudely ironic and self-aware attitude towards the literary act. Castel-Bloom, for example, titled her 1998 novel *Orly Castel-Bloom's New Book*. In Keret's work, the rejection of pathos took on a slightly different tone. The protagonists of his short-short stories are little people, often children, who suffer little defeats, endure many losses (but no dramatic or tragic ones) and achieve very few victories. Keret's hero is an unexceptional everyman, and there is no utopian horizon in his work: only the mediocre, childish life here on Earth.

In an era when the great conflicts seemed close to being resolved, there was no longer a place for prophet-writers (Oz, Yehoshua), dark writers (Shabtai) or writers who steadfastly believe in the power of aesthetics (Kenaz). Indeed, most of the works produced by the State Generation in the 1990s were relatively pallid, amplifying the sense that their role in Hebrew literature was over: the end of an era.

> **The novel is a quiet lamentation for the Hebrew culture of letters, which hangs by a thread**

*

All this changed in the first decade of the new millennium. If September 11 2001 marked, for the West, the end of the jubilant 1990s and a sobriety from the so-called "end of history", the shattering of the utopian vision in Israel was even harsher. The Second Intifada, which erupted in September 2000, crushed the messianic hopes pinned to the Oslo Accords for at least a generation. The Israeli–Palestinian conflict, it turned out, was more complex than many Israelis had believed. (It is worth remembering that some 1200 Israelis were murdered during the Second Intifada.)

Much as post-9/11 literature in the United States revolves around the return of seriousness and the marginalisation of postmodernism, Israeli literature in the 2000s had similar preoccupations. These were epitomised in the decade's exemplary book, Amos Oz's *A Tale of Love and Darkness* (2002). This fictionalised autobiography – widely viewed as Oz's finest book – marked the return of a member of the State Generation to centre stage after the exile imposed on him and his peers in the 1990s.

A Tale of Love and Darkness is, to my mind, a story of two perplexing questions. The visible question, noted by many readers and critics, is national-ideological: a scepticism of the justness of Zionism in the aftermath of the Second Intifada, and an acknowledgement that the roots of the Israeli–Palestinian conflict are in 1948, not 1967. Against this background, Oz was driven to autobiographical writing in an attempt to explain Zionism, to himself and to his readers, through his and his family's life experience. He portrays Zionism as an existential solution, a historical necessity for a tormented and persecuted people, rather than as a colonialist project executed by greedy, exploitative occupiers. But the hidden question – which many commentators did not observe – is intra-literary: a scepticism of the necessity of literature and "the author" in our age. That is the reason for the novel's compendious, nostalgic tone, which depicts the end of an era. The novel is not only a dirge for Zionism and its hazy future, however, but also a quiet lamentation for the Hebrew culture of letters, which hangs by a thread.

A Tale of Love and Darkness emerges in victory, which is responsible for some of its most exhilarating elements. The novel not only rehabilitates the Zionist narrative, but also resuscitates the moribund figure of "the author". Israel's national crisis, the Second Intifada, the gnawing at the Zionist narrative – all spurred Oz to investigate his family history. But these crises enabled him to re-establish his position as "the tribe magician", master of the national narrative, the author as superhero called to return from his dreary exile and heal the deep wounds that had emerged in the national narrative in his absence.

A Tale of Love and Darkness is, accordingly, an autobiographical novel and a literary bildungsroman – a portrait of the writer as a young man – and, furthermore, a historical novel that constitutes a sophisticated and subtle defence of Zionism. Thanks in large part to the influence of this work, but also because of the political and literary anxieties that led Oz to write it in the first place, those three genres dominated Israeli literary fiction in the 2000s. It was a decade that saw the publication of many autobiographical novels, such as Eyal Megged's *Woman Country* (2006) and Ronit Matalon's *The Sound of Our Footsteps* (2008); historical novels engaging with Zionism, including Amir Gutfreund's *The World a Moment Later* (2005) and Meir Shalev's *A Pigeon and a Boy* (2006); as well as novels that dwell on literature and the figure of the author, such as Benny Ziffer's *The Ascension of the Literary Editor* (2005) and Ofir Touché Gafla's *The Cataract in the Mind's Eye* (2005).

> *The literature of the second decade of the twenty-first century is typified, above all, by its "civic" character*

The domestic turn

The Israeli summer of 2011 was dominated by a massive social protest movement – the largest of its kind in the nation's history. In the same year, the Arab Spring and some of its less desirable outcomes (including the civil war in Syria) contributed to the most prominent political phenomenon in Israel in recent times: the continued regime of Benjamin Netanyahu.

These events formed the backdrop for the literature of the second decade of the twenty-first century, which is typified, above all, by its "civic" character. The emphasis on economic aspects of Israeli life and the erasure of the Israeli–Palestinian conflict from the Israeli agenda under Netanyahu (which has its own reasons and is certainly not exclusively Israel's "fault") inspired works that revolve around questions of class, status and social conflict. The prominent writers of the decade are markedly different from their predecessors (represented by the triumvirate of Oz, Yehoshua and Grossman), for whom "the conflict" was a major preoccupation in their work and their public engagement.

The work of Noa Yedlin, one of the most renowned Israeli writers of her generation, for example, is characterised by this "civic" engagement with money, status, real estate and similar concerns. Her 2013 novel, *House Arrest*, which won the Sapir Prize (Israel's most prestigious literary award), is the story of Elisheva Fogel, a professor of Jewish history and the deputy director of the fictional Theodore Hirsch Centre for Sustainable Peace, who is accused of embezzling millions of shekels from the centre. The story is told from the point of view of her son, Assa, a PhD who cannot find work in his field (critical research of New Age culture) and who feels like a failure in comparison with his overachieving mother. It is a novel about image versus substance. Is Elisheva as virtuous as she seems? Is it possible that a "square *yekke* with a Protestant work ethic", a "super-geek friend of the philharmonic", could have embezzled funds? Is a television series about a psychiatrist sent to help a community struck by tragedy – a series that Assa's younger brother, Amotz, is vying to take part in – a genuine therapeutic process or a spectacle? Does hiring a "media consultant" to handle the scandal imply an admission that what is important is mostly one's public image? Is Assa – a man battling New Age charlatans – about to discover that his own mother is a charlatan?

But in the new Israeli context, in which economic disparities are a greater concern than whether someone is a "dove" or a "hawk" on the Palestinian question, *House Arrest* is about the left-wing old guard's self-righteousness, about well-off progressive Ashkenazis who refuse to believe that one of their own could have committed a crime. Yedlin's oeuvre is part of a wave of criticism – indeed, self-criticism – levelled at the "white tribe" and the "old elites", a pursuit that has afflicted the Israeli left throughout the long Netanyahu era. But Yedlin's interests are broader than this, and she is a gifted satirist for whom issues of class, moral pretentiousness and moralism in general are home turf.

> **Thoughts that are not politically or "domestically" correct roil and gush beneath the surface**

Her 2019 novel, *People Like Us*, centres on Osnat and Dror, an Ashkenazi couple in their early forties who move to a fictitious neighbourhood in south Tel Aviv populated by mostly non-Ashkenazi Israelis and migrant workers. But the novel does not dwell on comfortable Ashkenazis' supposed racism towards different populations (Mizrahis, migrant workers and so on), or even on the disorientation experienced by an Ashkenazi couple in an unfamiliar environment. Rather, its most interesting content relates to the distress, cost and absurdities wrought by the moralistic, politically correct culture that increasingly dominates the lives of many Israelis – and certainly the protagonists' lives.

Dror and Osnat's ethos forbids them to voice "ugly" thoughts. As Dror says:

> How is a person measured? By how well he filters! By what he lets out! We have all kinds of things growing in our heads, they grow wildly, we have no control over it. But we can control what comes out of our mouth. So the fact that you have an evolutionary instinct to recoil from people who are different from you in all kinds of ways, that's one thing. That's natural. The question is, what sort of self-criticism do you apply?

This is an enlightened and respectable worldview. But Yedlin's satire illustrates that Dror also suffers from self-oppression – from an excess of the "self-criticism" he invokes – which results, for example, in his inability to voice the possibility that he might have inappropriate desires for other women (even in the example he gives Osnat to demonstrate his enlightened theory). Dror and Osnat's secular-liberal world has its own set of 613 commandments, both prescriptive and prohibitive. But beneath the strict policing of discourse and even thought, Yedlin shows the festering id. Thoughts that are not politically or "domestically" correct – as well as urges and aggressive inclinations – roil and gush beneath the surface.

*

This "civic" trend is notable in another significant contemporary writer, Dror Mishani, author of a series of detective novels about Inspector Avraham Avraham. Detective novels focus on domestic crime and violence, as opposed to the external violence of war. Their protagonists are police officers, not soldiers. Accordingly, Mishani's work engages with Israeli domestic tensions. His most recent book in the series, *Conviction* (2021), questions this domestic focus: Avraham's new boss thinks Avraham wants to switch jobs because he's convinced he belongs in "the big leagues" and that police work is inferior to that of other security organisations. The commander might be wrong about Avraham, but what he says seems to be true of the author himself. It is evident from this novel that Mishani is unsatisfied with the civic, familial, domestic nature of his detective stories, and does indeed wish to promote Avraham to "the big leagues" by reassigning him to the International Investigations Unit – meaning, as I see it, to the Grossman/Oz/Yehoshua league, where the main topic of discussion is what many believe serious Israeli literature should be about: the Israeli–Palestinian conflict.

> *The terror is convincing because it grows in the soil of ordinary life, which can be frightening and full of unpleasant surprises*

Mishani's previous novels, by contrast, focus on domestic and familial relations. A major psychological observation in *Three* (2018), the excellent novel that preceded *Conviction*, is this: life is frightening because human beings can be unpredictable, and the domestic can turn out to be *unheimlich* – "uncanny", as per Freud. The psychological terror – and this is Mishani's great achievement in *Three* – derives less from the serial killer and more from the awareness that "ordinary" people can turn on one another in non-criminal situations, such as within a marriage. The terror is convincing because it grows in the soil of ordinary life, which can be frightening and full of unpleasant surprises.

In his meticulous, believable and naturalistic detective novels, Mishani also touches on an issue which he explores more overtly in his academic and journalistic writing: the status of Mizrahis (Jews originally from Arab states). His detective, Avraham Avraham, and many of his other characters have Sephardi backgrounds, and indirectly attest to the standing of "Mizrahi ethnicities" in Israel. Mishani has noted how many of the Israel Police's employees are Mizrahis, which, he contends, explains its inferior reputation and status compared to the army, the Mossad and the Shin Bet, security apparatuses with an Ashkenazi character and, accordingly, far greater prestige.

*

The most prominent young Israeli writer (in fiction writing, early fifties is still considered "young") is Maya Arad. I remember being surprised when she mentioned, early in her literary career, that her Israeli role model was Aharon Megged (1920–2016). Not the aforementioned triumvirate, not even Kenaz the aesthete, or the Schopenhauer-esque Shabtai, but Megged, a prolific writer with a slightly dull image. In other words, Arad did not strive to emulate the prophet-writers, but the professional ones. Her diverse oeuvre avoids "classic" Israeli topics such as the Israeli–Palestinian conflict and the Holocaust, instead dealing with "minor" issues such as social status, the desires and anxieties of relationships, and parenthood.

Arad is noted for moving her characters through various tribulations, at the end of which they attain sobriety from their self-delusion and overly ambitious or romantic fantasies. In *The Maiden of Kazan* (2015), she walks the protagonist, Idit, along a via dolorosa, from her dream of marriage – which shatters – to a dream of motherhood – which also collapses – and finally to a dream of adoption – which at first seems doomed as well. Alongside her disillusionment when it comes to romance and motherhood, Idit eventually recognises her gloomy economic prospects:

> Once, in her prior life, Idit looked down on people with overdrawn bank accounts. What was so difficult about planning ahead a little? Take her: she earned a teacher's salary, but she got along just fine. Why couldn't other people? But now she'd been forced to take a cut in her income, yet she was shelling out huge sums on daycare, babysitters and therapists.

Shortly afterwards, the moment of truth and terror approaches: Idit will have to leave Tel Aviv!

Many of Arad's characters, like her, are Israelis living in the United States, having relocated temporarily, permanently or temporarily-that-became-permanently. This is a significant Israeli sociological phenomenon, although Arad's primary interest is in the comedy of manners.

The anti-prophetic and antipathetic mood of the young generation in Israeli fiction is tied to its affection for satire. In addition to Yedlin's work and some of Arad's, other examples of fine satirical writing include Matan Hermoni's *Spielvogel, Spielvogel* (2019) and Yirmi Pinkus's *Petty Business* (2012). Even a writer far removed from satire, David Grossman, surprised readers with his excellent 2014 novel about a stand-up comic, *A Horse Walks Into a Bar*.

The future of the Israeli novel

Most of the writers I've mentioned as part of this current generation (Yedlin, Mishani, Arad) were born in the 1970s. Their cohort includes Shimon Adaf, Yaniv Iczkovits, Sarah Blau, Nir Baram, Eshkol Nevo, Dorit Rabinyan and Sami Berdugo. It also includes two authors, Assaf Inbari and Dror Burstein, who ask weighty questions regarding the novel's role in our age.

Burstein was at his height when depicting the crisis of literature, as he did most explicitly in his early novel *Murderers* (2006). Its protagonist, Shaul Robinson, despondent over his failed literary career, fakes his own death in the hope that he may finally earn recognition as a dead poet. When the ruse fails, he acknowledges that Hebrew poetry has no future ("Hebrew literature has one disease, which is that it is written in a language understood by only a few people, equivalent to the population of a small town in America or a mid-sized Russian *sovkhoz*. But it has aspirations.") and turns instead to translating the finest twentieth-century Hebrew poetry into English. One by one, every publisher in London rejects his manuscript ("Your Bialik in English is the poetry of a somewhat skilled theology student, your Uri Zvi Greenberg in English is a pretentious working class poet from the East End ... your Avidan in English is nothing more than a megalomaniac rich kid studying literature at Oxford who knows how to rhyme.") But things do not end there: the desperate Robinson translates these Hebrew classics back into Hebrew from his own English translations, and is astonished to find that Israeli publishers, not recognising the originals, are happy to publish the work as original Hebrew poetry.

One element of Burstein's wild humour is his virtuosic impersonations of classical writers. No one escapes his pastiche in *Murderers*: Franz Kafka, Nathan Alterman, Agnon, Gnessin,

Thomas Bernhard, Meir Wieseltier, A.B. Yehoshua and, of course, Yaakov Shabtai, in whose "style" large parts of the book are written. Some of these imitations appear without warning, occurring organically in the text and prodding the reader into a delightful game of "guess the original", but others are explicit, leading the reader to the novel's central theme, which is the near-impossibility of writing anything original in an era in which "everything has already been written". But, as it turns out, Robinson is not the only literary thief in this novel, and it is through the other "thieves" that Burstein investigates the question of originality.

From this awareness of a crisis in contemporary literature, Burstein seemed to increasingly turn his back on fiction and the novel. He has since focused on essayistic writing driven by ecological post-humanist concerns – for example, in books about animals, and works inspired by Far Eastern doctrines, Spinoza-esque pantheism and environmental New Age philosophies. Burstein's rejection of fiction and his choice of themes strike me as a profound reflection of the zeitgeist, despite my distaste for the post-humanist ideology they evince.

*

Another interesting – but more positive – way of thinking about the future of the novel is reflected in Assaf Inbari's three books (billed as novels, though they are not unequivocally so, as will become apparent). In *Home* (2009), Inbari seems to have invented a new genre: the biography of a place. The book features "characters" and "protagonists", but its central character is Kibbutz Afikim in the Jordan Valley.

Employing what is clearly exhaustive research (aided by the kibbutz members' yen for self-documentation), Inbari relates the story from beginning to end: birth – when a group of men and women in their twenties establish the Ha'Shomer Hatzair movement in post-revolutionary Russia; their migration to pre-state Israel as part of the Third Aliya; ideological arguments; collective labour in various parts of the country (building the city of Afula, for example); settling near Lake Tiberias, and later in the Jordan Valley; the War of Independence and holding the Syrians at bay; the rift in the kibbutz movement over the USSR; the prosperity of the 1950s and early 1960s, when Afikim was one of the three largest kibbutzim in Israel; the emergence of the first ideological cracks; the "reversal" of the 1977 elections, in which Likud ended the Labor Party's long reign; the enormous losses in the stock market and the recovery program imposed on the kibbutzim in the 1980s; privatisation – death. These broad strokes are filled in with nuanced details, including a close examination of the fissures.

Inbari finds that the first crack emerged as early as the 1950s, when the kibbutz began allocating vouchers to members so that they could purchase supplies according to their preference. The second occurred during the transition from direct democracy (the kibbutz assembly) to representative democracy. Other fractures were prompted by the distribution of reparations from Germany and the resulting inequities, and the introduction of capitalist management methods to the kibbutz's profitable plywood factory. But Inbari's meticulous research does not make the book a tedious historic study, nor detract from the joy of reading it.

Inbari's two other novels, *The Tank* (2018) and *The Red Book* (2022), are also documentary novels par excellence, each dealing with a historical episode in the annals of Zionism, and in particular the history of the Israeli labour movement. But it would be misleading to characterise Inbari as a writer who dwells in the past.

His work displays profound and fruitful ideas about the nature of the novel in contemporary life, and offers a fascinating answer to the question of how to preserve the genre's vitality in contemporary cultural conditions.

In an essay published in 2002, Inbari advocates a return to a fiction of action – rather than one of emotional deliberations and descriptions – that echoes the Biblical language of action. It seems to me that Inbari is trying to resuscitate fiction while drawing inspiration from the earliest manifestations of Western prose: classical Greek and Roman historians, alongside sections of the Bible. Inbari writes like Tacitus or Thucydides, or the author of the Book of Samuel. His viewpoint is retrospective (as Hegel observed, "the owl of Minerva spreads its wings only with the falling of dusk"; in other words, we understand the past only when it is over – when it becomes a story with a beginning, a middle and an end), and he writes about the real deeds of real people who operated within and contributed to important historical developments. The members of Kibbutz Afikim in *Home*, the War of Independence soldiers in *The Tank* and the three leaders of the Israeli left in *The Red Book* are all depicted in laconic, fast-paced prose, and the vibrant result is evidence that important Israeli fiction is still being written.

> *If no substantial new Hebrew texts are written, Israelis will return to the scriptures*

*

Will the future of Hebrew literature produce works equal to those of the State Generation? The structural and economic conditions of literature in Israel are insecure, partly due to the oligopoly that has emerged in the market, with conflicting interests and overlapping ownership among the major publishers and bookstore chains. Furthermore, there are too many books published in Israel today, many of them funded by the authors, a phenomenon that makes it difficult to single out important works. And, finally, book reading has lost significant ground to other leisure activities, such as television and social media. I believe that a non-religious (though not necessarily "secular") Hebrew culture requires meaningful texts. Other media (such as television, which has seen a flourishing Israeli industry in the past two decades) cannot take the unique place of literature. The innate abstractness and, for want of a better term, spiritualism of belles-lettres, and the unique expertise of literature in portraying what E.M. Forster termed people's "secret lives", are unparalleled in other media. If no substantial new Hebrew texts are written, Israelis will return to the scriptures. Some already have. It is not only nature that does not permit a vacuum – the same is true for culture.

History

The curse on Spinoza

Steven Nadler

On 27 July 1656, the Portuguese-Jewish community of Amsterdam permanently expelled one of its young, rebellious members. The community's *parnassim* (lay leaders or directors) could not possibly have anticipated the remarkable historical legacy of what they did that day.

The only remaining documentation of the event is preserved in the *Livro dos Acordos da Naçao e Ascamot*, the community's record book, now in the Portuguese-Jewish Archives of the Amsterdam Municipal Archives:

> The *Senhores* of the *ma'amad* [board of directors] make known to you that having for some time reports of the bad opinions and acts of Baruch de Spinoza, they have endeavored by various means and promises to turn him from his bad ways. But being unable to effect any remedy, on the contrary, each day receiving more information about the abominable heresies which he practiced and taught and about the monstrous deeds which he performed ... the said Espinoza should be banned and separated [*enhermado e apartado*] from the Nation of Israel, as they now put him under *herem* [*poin em herem*] with the following *herem*:

> With the judgment of the angels and with that of the saints, we put under *herem* [*enhermamos*], ostracize, and curse and damn Baruch de Espinoza … Cursed be he by day and cursed be he by night; cursed be he when he lies down and cursed be he when he rises up. Cursed be he when he goes out and cursed be he when he comes in. *Adonai* will not forgive him.

With this writ of *herem*, the 23-year-old Bento (or Baruch) de Spinoza was formally and irrevocably cast out of the Talmud Torah congregation.

Spinoza's parents were former "conversos" – Jews who had been forced to convert to Catholicism in Spain and Portugal in the fifteenth and sixteenth centuries (although many continued to practise Judaism in secret). His parents fled the violence of the Portuguese Inquisition, and by the early 1620s the family were settled in Amsterdam, where they joined the Sephardi community that, just a few decades earlier, had found safe haven under Dutch toleration. At the time of his *herem*, Spinoza and his younger brother Gabriel were running their late father's importing firm. Once the *herem* was pronounced, however, he had to leave his business and his family behind.

The punishment Spinoza received is commonly called an "excommunication", and translations typically have the *parnassim* declaring that they are "excommunicating" Spinoza. However, the directors of the Portuguese-Jewish community seem to have gone out of their way to avoid using the term "excommunicate". More than forty of the community's *herem* documents have survived, including Spinoza's, and all prefer some form of the phrase "put under *herem*" – even, it seems, taking the root letters of the Hebrew (h, r, m) and inventing a Portuguese verb: *enhermar*, to put under *herem*.

Perhaps this community of Spanish and Portuguese émigrés avoided using such a Catholic-loaded term as "excommunication". After all, Judaism does not have any communion. Moreover, a *herem* typically was more extensive than Catholic excommunication. It did not merely remove the right to participate in liturgical practices (such as serving in a minyan or being called to the Torah). A *herem* affected practically all religious, social and economic aspects of an individual's life. Financial dealings or even conversations with a person under *herem* were prohibited, and so the individual could not engage in ordinary social and business affairs. He or she was cut off from being an active member of the community – persona non grata in the fullest sense.

As well, unlike Catholic excommunication, punishment by *herem* was not only for religious offences. Amsterdam's Sephardim did employ the *herem* for religious and devotional matters, such as attendance at synagogue, following the dietary laws of *kashrut* and observance of holidays. But a Portuguese Jew in Amsterdam could also earn a *herem* for more mundane transgressions, such as buying meat from an Ashkenazi butcher. Then there were ethical and social regulations: one could be banned for gambling or for lewd behaviour in the streets, or for marrying in secret, without parental consent and not in the presence of a rabbi. One could be banned for failing to pay communal taxes, for shady business dealings or for showing disrespect to a member of the *ma'amad*. Women were forbidden, under threat of *herem*, to cut the hair of non-Jewish women, and

> *The directors of the Portuguese-Jewish community seem to have gone out of their way to avoid using the term "excommunicate"*

members of the community were warned not to engage non-Jews in theological discussions. Sexual relations between Jews and non-Jews were also prohibited.

Spinoza's *herem*, however, was more vehement and more furious than any other proclaimed by the *parnassim*. No other *herem* issued by the Amsterdam Sephardi community contains the wrath and curses directed at Spinoza. More typical was the *herem* in 1639 against Isaac de Peralta for assaulting a rabbi in the street. De Peralta got off relatively easy: the *ma'amad* merely declared him "under *herem*" and decreed that "no one shall talk or deal with him. Only family and other members of his household may talk with him." After four days, De Peralta begged forgiveness and paid a fine of sixty guilders, and the *herem* was lifted. For Spinoza, by contrast, there seems to be no hope of reconciliation, no amends that could be made to have the *herem* lifted. Spinoza was out for good.

*

The obvious question, of course, is *why* Spinoza was banned with such extreme prejudice. Neither the *herem* nor any document from the period tells us exactly what his "bad opinions and acts" were, nor what "abominable heresies" or "monstrous deeds" he is alleged to have taught and practised. Spinoza never refers to this period of his life in his extant letters, and does not offer his correspondents, or us, any clues about why he was expelled. There is thus a bit of a mystery here.

Odette Vlessing, former curator of Amsterdam's Portuguese-Jewish archives, has argued that Spinoza's *herem* was related to machinations he undertook to avoid financial obligations. In March 1656, just four months before the ban, Spinoza initiated drastic steps to relieve himself of debts he had inherited along with the estate of his late father, Michael. He took advantage of a Dutch law that protected underaged children who had lost their parents. Because he was a year and a few months shy of his twenty-fifth birthday, he was still legally a minor. Spinoza filed a petition with the civil authorities and was declared an orphan, which allowed him to avoid paying his father's debts.

According to Vlessing, Spinoza's legal manoeuvre threatened the Jewish community's reputation for trustworthiness in business affairs – something it counted on heavily in its relations with the Dutch. And it was not only Dutch creditors on his father's estate whose expectations would not be met: Spinoza was also shirking commitments to fellow Portuguese-Jewish merchants. In other words, Spinoza, the son of a one-time *parnas*, was going over the heads of the sitting *parnassim* and putting Dutch law above communal regulations (which stipulated that business disputes should be handled within the community) and Jewish law, and this, as Vlessing sees it, was a serious offence indeed. "Michael Spinoza's financial disaster and Baruch Spinoza's appeal for release from his father's estate on the grounds of minority," she argues, "must have shaken the Jewish community."

These were not sentiments likely to endear one to the rabbis and lay leaders of a Jewish community in the seventeenth century

Vlessing makes a very interesting case. However, the text of Spinoza's *herem* suggests, rather explicitly, that his offence was more than just a matter of business and financial irregularities, or even communal behaviour that violated Jewish law. After all, the document refers to his "abominable heresies" and "bad opinions". Vlessing insists that "Spinoza was not excommunicated on account of his philosophical ideas". However, given the wording of the ban, not to mention its length, its vitriol, its uniqueness and its finality, it is hard to avoid the conclusion that it was precisely his ideas that occasioned the final and irrevocable ostracism.

Further evidence is found in reports that two Spanish visitors to Amsterdam in 1658 made to the Inquisition upon their return to their homeland. The Augustinian monk Tomás Solano y Robles and a military captain named Miguel Pérez de Maltranilla both told the inquisitors that in Amsterdam they had met someone named Spinoza, and that he claimed that he had once been observant of Jewish law but, after a "change of mind", was expelled from the community because of his views on God, the soul and the law. He said he had, in the eyes of the congregation, "reached the point of atheism".

These are rather vague remarks. But if we take as our guide Spinoza's philosophical writings – on which he began working within just a few years of the *herem* – it is not difficult to imagine the kinds of things he must have been thinking, and probably saying, around late 1655 and early 1656.

In *Ethics*, Spinoza's philosophical masterpiece begun in the early 1660s, he basically denies that the human soul is immortal in the sense that a person enjoys a life after death. Thus, there is nothing to hope for or fear in terms of eternal reward or punishment. Indeed, Spinoza insists, the notion of God acting as a judge who dispenses rewards and punishments is based on absurd, superstitious anthropomorphising of the deity. In truth, God is simply the infinite, eternal substance in which all things exist and, as such, is identical with Nature itself. Everything that exists and everything that happens follows from "God or Nature" with absolute necessity. The notion of a supernatural, providential God is nothing but a pernicious fiction.

Then there are Spinoza's views on the Bible. One of the primary lessons of the *Theological-Political Treatise*, which he published anonymously to great alarm in 1670, is that the Hebrew Bible is not of divine origin. Rather, it is the work of a number of human authors, writing in different historical periods and political contexts; and the text we now have is the product of editorial work and historical transmission. As for the laws of the Torah, these, he insists, are no longer binding on or valid for latter-day Jews. With the end of the Jewish commonwealth and the destruction of the Temple, most of the 613 *mitzvot* have lost their raison d'être.

These were not sentiments likely to endear one to the rabbis and lay leaders of a Jewish community in the seventeenth century – especially the Amsterdam Sephardi community in the decades after its founding. Because these were conversos or descendants of conversos who, for generations, had been cut off from Jewish life – its laws, ceremonies and texts – the rabbis and directors of the Talmud Torah congregation had to work especially hard to educate these immigrants in the ways of normative Judaism and keep them on the straight and narrow. They could not tolerate deviations from Jewish practice or the rejection of central Jewish doctrines. The denial of the divinity of the Torah, of a personal God and the miracles he is supposed to have performed, and of Jewish law would all have been seen as threats to the orthodoxy and unity of the community. The rejection of the immortality of the soul, in particular, would have been taken very seriously by a community whose Judaism still reflected the Catholic heritage of many of its members. There may also have been some fear among the congregation's leaders that all of these views could have offended their Dutch Calvinist hosts, and thus threatened the refuge they had found in Holland.

Spinoza seems not to have been very bothered by his ban. He had almost certainly, by this point, lost his Jewish faith and commitment to Jewish life. We can regard the *herem* as perhaps the defining moment of his life. But according to one early biography, written shortly after his death, his response was rather cool:

> All the better; they do not force me to do anything that I would not have done of my own accord if I did not dread scandal. But, since they want it that way, I enter gladly on the path that is opened to me, with the consolation that my departure will be more innocent than was the exodus of the early Hebrews from Egypt. ▤

Community

A community to celebrate: The Jews of Singapore

Michael Vatikiotis

On a street in Singapore named after the famous Battle of Waterloo, South-East Asia's oldest synagogue sits not far from a Hindu temple, a Catholic church and a Buddhist shrine. Waterloo Street is emblematic of the distinct form of pluralism that characterises much of South-East Asian society.

Unlike old European notions of social diversity, with their ideals of integration and assimilation, pluralism in Asia allows religious or ethnic communities to maintain their identities, to live side by side and mix, rather than combine. In the colonial era, this absence of a collective identity made for an efficient labour force; in modern times, the legacy has been that communities have preserved their customs and that people of different ethnicities and faiths have been able to peacefully coexist.

And so it is not uncommon in the region to find churches situated alongside Hindu or Buddhists temples, close to mosques – and, yes, synagogues too. The modern pluralist society in South-East Asia is enshrined in law. The right to worship different faiths and speak different tongues is foundational, if not always respected. There might be periodic friction, and majorities who feel the need to assert themselves at the expense of minorities, especially when politicians are prone to using religious orthodoxy and intolerance to drum up votes. Yet by and large the pluralist society has endured peacefully. The Jews of Singapore are no exception, but for many years very few people knew their history and their unique provenance.

This changed recently, with the opening of a modest museum that puts their record on public display for the first time. "The fact that there is a Jewish community in Singapore is fresh news to Singaporeans," said Laure Lau, the Singaporean curator of the Jews of Singapore Museum, which opened in 2021.

Perhaps the most interesting aspect of the Jewish community in Singapore – the oldest and largest in South-East Asia – is its Middle Eastern roots. The first Jews who settled in Singapore, and in other parts of South-East Asia, were from Baghdad. This community, who trace their history back more than 2000 years to ancient Iraq, migrated eastwards in search of trade, much as other Arabs did from the Arabian Peninsula and the Levant.

Arab merchants, riding the trade winds out of ports along the Indian coast, brought Islam to Java and Sumatra in the ninth century. Baghdadi Jews joined these same trade routes. By the eighteenth century, Jewish traders had established themselves in the emerging colonial port cities of Cochin, Bombay, Madras and Calcutta. It was a short hop from there to the new commercial centres of Rangoon and Singapore, which grew fast under British colonial rule in the mid-nineteenth century.

Here these Baghdadi Jews initially rubbed shoulders with other Arab traders and migrants. They spoke a common language, wore the same dress and ate pretty much the same kinds of food. But as British rule strengthened, they shed their outward Arab appearance and adopted anglicised names – Mashal becoming Marshall, Seleiman Solomon, and Bagnani Benjamin. Following the opening of the Suez Canal in 1869, many Jews arrived in Singapore from other places – Europe, as well as Egypt and the Levant.

But the predominantly orthodox Sephardi tradition of the Iraqi core of the community remained, and survives today in the contemporary Jewish community of around 2000 people. The Maghain Aboth Synagogue on Waterloo Street was completed in 1878, and so is the oldest in South-East Asia; it was made a national monument by Singapore in 1998. The building's design was neoclassical, popular in the colonial period. A second-storey gallery overlooking the synagogue floor, and dedicated for women to worship, was added later.

The ornamental chamber that houses the synagogue's Torah scrolls (known as *Hekhal* or *Aron Hakodesh*) is home to dozens of Torahs dating back to the early 1900s. Two are currently on loan to Singapore's Asian Civilisations Museum. The U-shaped layout is classically Sephardi. A second synagogue, Chesed-El, was opened in 1905 in nearby Oxley Rise. Supported by the prominent Iraqi-Jewish trader and generous philanthropist Sir Manasseh Meyer (1846–1930), the synagogue continues to serve the community today.

"The jewel of the community is Baghdadi"

"The jewel of community is Baghdadi," said Chief Rabbi Mordechai Abergel. He pointed out that until World War II, the community was strongly anchored to the Iraqi homeland; its rabbis were sent from Iraq and were spiritually directed from Iraq. To this day, the Jewish Welfare Board includes fourth-generation descendants of Iraqi families. Of course, Jews from other parts of the world settled in Singapore too. Today's community includes

Europeans, Americans, Australians, South Africans and a sizeable Israeli contingent.

World War II was an inflection point for the community, as it was for many other minorities in Singapore. The trauma of the Japanese occupation, the poverty of post-war South-East Asia and the opening of migration routes to Australia and other Commonwealth countries saw many Jews leave Singapore.

Those who remained grew up with Singapore as it started to prosper again and gained independence in 1963. They have strongly identified as Singaporean. One prominent member of the community, David Marshall, was one of the island republic's pioneering leaders. Marshall's parents, who were merchants, had emigrated from Baghdad; he was raised in the Orthodox Sephardi tradition, but like other wealthy members of the community he attended elite English-language schools in Singapore. The Iraqi Jews were mainly in business, and some became prominent professionals. They went to local schools and rubbed shoulders with Singapore's emerging leaders. They are pillars of the Singapore community, not just as Jews but as Singaporeans, no longer Arab but Asian.

The museum tells their story, really for the first time. Through a combination of illustrated panels and mixed audio and visual media, the visitor learns that many of the early Iraqi migrants were poor journeymen who came as dock workers and labourers. There were rich members of the community who moved in colonial circles and went to good schools, which helped mainstream the Jewish community as Singaporean. The poorer members lived in the old Mahalla, in the southern part of the city. They baked bread and made cheese or delivered kosher food for the richer members of the community, but otherwise there was little social interaction beyond the synagogue.

Singapore is famously food-obsessed, and curator Laure Lau has linked the museum to the small supermarket that sells imported kosher products as part of the recently renovated complex built around the main synagogue.

The museum gives the community a new level of exposure – what was before a purely oral tradition, handed down from one generation to the next, is now bound in a glossy coffee table book written in 2007 by the American scholar Joan Bieder, and emblazoned on pictorial panels that line the museum's walls. The museum is very much a coming out for a community, which, like other religious minorities, such as the Armenians and Shiite Muslim Ismailis, has kept a low profile.

Perhaps helping to bring about this change to this most traditional Sephardi community is the modest but charismatic figure of Rabbi Abergel. Of Moroccan origin, he grew up in Europe. A member of the US-based Chabad-Lubavitch movement, Rabbi Abergel has steered the community towards a more inclusive and outgoing path since the mid-1990s. His wife, Simcha, has established a Jewish school in Singapore.

> *They are pillars of the Singapore community, not just as Jews but as Singaporeans, no longer Arab but Asian*

The community's modern challenges are similar, in a way, to those of the past – to broaden its appeal to a wider Jewish cohort living and working in Singapore, and to integrate with others. The Sir Manasseh Meyer International School, for example, is open to non-Jews and is one of the more affordable international schools in Singapore. With the help of various trusts, financial support is provided for families on a needs basis.

But according to Rabbi Abergel, the challenge, as in the post-war years, is that Singapore's population is again transient and in flux. "We have gone through dips before," he says resignedly. "In 1997 [during the Asian Financial Crisis] more than fifty families left Singapore."

In this respect, the Jews of Singapore Museum can be an asset as the composition of the community in Singapore morphs and changes. It directs people to a little-known history and emphatically declares how comfortable the Jewish community is about its heritage. "The local Iraqi Jews of Singapore have intermarried into the wider Jewish community and made other connections," says Rabbi Abergel. "It shows how the only way for [this] community to survive was to be less cliquish and graft on other elements so it can grow."

Quite so. In keeping with the traditional notion of the pluralist society in South-East Asia, Singapore's communities of Middle Eastern heritage – whether Armenian, Zoroastrian, Yemeni or Jewish – have retained much of their distinctive identity and character. The future does hold some uncertainty, though. After a long period in which migrants from all over the world settled in Singapore, enriching as well as diversifying the island republic's Jewish community, the government today is feeling some domestic pressure to limit the flow of inward migrants. For some it is harder to stay long-term, and these days Rabbi Abergel, in addition to welcoming newcomers to his flock, is frequently bidding farewell to those departing. ▰

Reviews

Inside the Old City of Jerusalem
Irris Makler

Nine Quarters of Jerusalem:
A New Biography of the Old City
Matthew Teller
Profile Books (UK)/ Other Press (US)

The classical Jewish texts speak about "*Yerushalayim shel mala*" – celestial or holy Jerusalem – and "*Yerushalayim shel mata*" – earthly or lower Jerusalem. The city, tethered somewhere between heaven and earth, seems to thrum at a higher frequency due to all the prayers directed towards it, and British journalist and travel writer Matthew Teller captures its duality in his new book, *Nine Quarters of Jerusalem*.

Part travelogue, part in-depth historical tour, *Nine Quarters* is cleverly structured and well written. It is also both funny and angry. Teller doesn't live here, but he's been bitten by the Jerusalem bug.

"Jerusalem is not my city and never will be. That said, there has hardly been a year in my life in which it has not played a part," he writes. He visits often, has relatives here and, in a note at the end, says he wants to amplify the narratives he didn't hear when he visited as a child with his Jewish family. On that first trip as a boy, Teller was overwhelmed by the riot of colours and scents.

"All my life cumin has meant my first trip to Jerusalem … For years, I put cumin in everything. I was really putting Jerusalem in everything."

The book begins with an old map, which, Teller argues, leads directly to the present-day political situation. It sets him on a historical quest to investigate how the Old City came to be divided into its current four quarters: Christian, Jewish, Muslim and Armenian. Teller explains that by the 1800s, Ottoman Jerusalem was a small, messy, organic, mostly Muslim city, with no named quarters but a multitude of neighbourhoods. (The population proportion remains much the same today: over 80 per cent of the present-day Old City's 36,000 or so inhabitants are Muslim.) "All throughout its long, long history, it was never divided into four, neat, religious quarters. Until the British arrived."

Teller's thesis is that Jerusalem was boxed up – drawn and quartered, if you like – by nineteenth-century British mapmakers in order to legitimise British political claims to the city and the wider region. Teller appears nostalgic for nineteenth-century Ottoman Jerusalem, and the British actions infuriate him, especially those of the man he identifies as the main culprit, one Reverend George Williams – or, as he dubs him, the Reverend George ridiculous Williams. "For almost two hundred years, virtually the entire world has accepted the ill-informed, dismissive judgmentalism of a jejune Old Etonian missionary as representing enduring fact about the social make-up of Jerusalem. It's shameful," Teller writes.

Teller argues that the British maps facilitated seeing Jerusalem as significant primarily to Christians and Jews, and underpinned British policy during its rule over Mandatory Palestine from 1917 to 1948. The maps supported the "poisonous old narrative of divide and rule", he concludes. "British colonial rule furthered the ambitions of Palestine's Jewish communities over all others. Jerusalem wasn't always a zero-sum game, but Britain made it so, in our time."

Teller pounds the Old City on foot – "the only way to know it is to walk it" – to meet the varied communities which still share this tiny space, the "Nine Quarters" of his title. It's a conceit that allows him to show us the Old City from the ground up, focusing on little-known groups such as its Indian and West African communities, its Dom Gypsies, its Sufi mystics, its Ethiopian, Syriac and Armenian churches, its Karaite Jewish-Muslim hybrids. Whenever he reaches a historically significant spot, he describes the people living there today. It's a very satisfying structure. He begins by following the Stations of the Cross along the Via Dolorosa, the Way of Sorrows, which Christians believe (as, to my surprise, does Teller) is built on the actual route Jesus walked to his crucifixion.

At the fourth station, where Jesus met his mother, there is a building which was Jerusalem's swankiest hotel in the nineteenth century, managed by a Jew from Belarus who converted to Christianity. Mark Twain stayed there for two nights in 1867, a visit he wrote up in his celebrated travel book *The Innocents Abroad*. In the 1980s, the building was bought by Ariel Sharon, then an Israeli general and politician. Though he subsequently sold it, many locals still refer to it as Ariel Sharon's house.

The seventh station, where Jesus fell for a second time, is today one of the busiest spots in the Old City. Here, Motassem al Amad sells the best halva in town. (Teller reveals the secret ingredient, soapwort.) "Daughters of Jerusalem, weep not for me but for yourselves and your children," said Jesus at the eighth station, where

Teller interviews an Arab woman selling vegetables grown in her village, situated between Jerusalem and Bethlehem. He calls her Umm Ahmed to protect her identity because, as a Palestinian from the West Bank, her presence is illegal under Israeli rules. Her story is a window into the restrictions on Palestinian daily life in Jerusalem and its environs.

Teller reflects on the alchemy of being a tourist in the souk, where you remain invisible as long as you're in motion. "Stop and it's as if you materialise. You solidify from vapour to customer." Every visitor to the souk will recognise that molecular change. Despite the hard sell on the part of vendors, a source of complaint for generations, visitors keep returning. Perhaps my favourite explanation comes from an Islamic religious scholar, who says living here is "like having the right plug. It lets you plug into the energy source."

After the Stations of the Cross, Teller takes us to each Old City gate in turn, where the stories he unearths make the book sing. At the Lions' Gate, he finds a group of Dom – gypsies originally from India, who today mostly live in Turkey and Iran; about 20,000 live in Gaza and the West Bank, and some 600 in the Old City. Teller meets Amoun Sleem, a woman working to preserve the Dom culture. The Dom are neither Palestinian nor Israeli, she explains, which makes them destined to remain eternal outsiders. "Israelis dismiss the Dom as Arabs but Arabs dismiss them as 'Nawar' [black]," he writes.

From there, Teller goes to nearby Aladdin Street. This allows him to tell the backstory of the eighteenth-century Syrian storyteller Hanna Diyab, author of *Aladdin and His Magic Lamp* (and *Ali Baba and the Forty Thieves*). He was only credited as author after his memoir was unearthed in the Vatican library in the 1990s, more than 250 years after the French orientalist Antoine Galland published Diyab's folktales under his own name. (Such historical digressions are one of the joys of this book.)

Teller visits two buildings on Aladdin Street that house Muslims originally from West Africa. Their ancestors began visiting in the 1400s, after completing the Hajj to Mecca. They were not slaves, and received better treatment than other Africans. Some stayed on. Around 200 people – twenty-eight families – still live there today. These "Afro-Palestinians" are more integrated and accepted than the Dom Gypsies, which Teller argues may be because they identify with the Palestinians and take part in the Resistance against Israel.

No gate can evade Teller, even one that is sealed shut. The Golden Gate, possibly the grandest of the Old City gates, has almost never been opened. "A gate that is not a gate. A gate through which no one can pass. A gate that, in three thousand years, has only even been open for momentous encounters with the Divine. The Golden Gate is irresistibly mysterious." He surmises that Muslim rulers sealed it shut because of its importance to Jewish and Christian worship. "Do not be frivolous or lighthearted when you near it, warns the Mishnah ... Prepare yourself for the fateful day it opens again."

Teller interviews Armenian rock stars, and a Coptic Christian tattooist whom he meets after spotting the sign "Razzouk Tattoo. Since 1300". Wassim Razzouk, president of the Holy Land Bikers Motorcycle Club, is the twenty-seventh generation in the family business. Since tattooing is for the most part avoided by both Muslims and Jews, Christians have cornered the market. Their main customers are pilgrims, and Razzouk sees the process as akin to baptism, a physical act that leaves a spiritual mark. For a

Christian pilgrim to Jerusalem to be tattooed by a non-Christian would be "like buying a fake Rolex", he says.

"Sell your cleverness and buy bewilderment," wrote the poet Rumi, advice relevant to pilgrims of all faiths, and especially to Sufi mystics, another group Teller discovers living in the Old City and is sympathetic to and fascinated by. But he remains furious with the officials of British Mandatory Palestine. He writes scathingly about architect Charles Robert Ashbee. "I've never felt so pagan and repelled in my life," Ashbee wrote home when he arrived in Jerusalem in 1918, before he set about trying to change the city into a place that would suit him better. "Ashbee's whim was law. And Jerusalem was about to get that whim right between the eyes," says Teller. He disapproves of Ashbee's twee English vision of how Jerusalem should look, and what sort of city it should be.

"In Ashbee's mind, it seems, all humanity yearned to live in a nice, neat little town in southern England," Teller fulminates. He argues that Ashbee's aesthetic isolated and commodified the Old City, creating an "Arts and Crafts vision of an idealised medieval walled city. Our twenty-first-century experience is rooted in, and framed by, a regressive nineteenth-century British rural sensibility."

Teller also blames this philosophy for the British destruction of a grand Turkish clocktower at the Jaffa Gate, which he describes as "geo-political triumphalism dressed up as good taste". In fact, the British destroyed the tower twice – first the much-loved original, in 1922, and then, twelve years later, the tower they themselves built after the huge outcry following the demolition of the first. Teller sees such an approach as both high-handed and harmful to the Old City's Muslim population, and goes on to argue that many Mandate-era policies, from the law that all buildings must be clad in local limestone, known as "Jerusalem stone", to the division between the walled Old City and the modern city beyond, still form the basis of Israeli planning policy today.

Teller, who is himself British, places British "perfidy" centre stage but pays little attention to the failures of the Ottomans, who had ruled for the previous 400 years. Most historians describe Turkish rule as neglectful and exploitative. The Ottomans built few roads, bridges, sewers or irrigation channels, while imposing crippling taxes. This kept the land barren, and the local population poor. When British historian Alexander W. Kinglake crossed the Jordan River in 1834, he used its only bridge, built originally by the Romans. In *The Innocents Abroad,* written some thirty years later, Twain describes a "desolate country whose soil is rich enough, but is given over wholly to weeds – a silent, mournful expanse". Twain even wonders whether this devastation is the fulfilment of a Biblical curse. (Teller dismisses Twain's descriptions because his book is "not reportage" and calls him a "comedian on tour", as though an author can't be both funny and accurate.)

Ottoman neglect and local poverty were also factors in the success of the newly formed Zionist movement, explaining the readiness of absentee landlords to sell tracts of swamp or desert land to Jewish philanthropists in the nineteenth century. In this context, Teller protests too much: British maps and support from Mandate officials were certainly not the only reasons the Zionists prospered.

Still, he is an impassioned narrator with an eye for the absurd. One of my favourite stories is of a mournful Iraqi Sufi, Sufyan al Thawri, who arrived in Jerusalem in the eighth century. He was renowned for wearing black and weeping as he prayed at the Dome of the Rock. When he managed to stop crying, he declared that life's greatest pleasure was eating bananas there. Teller can't resist adding a Jerusalem geographer's description of bananas from two centuries later: "A fruit in the form of the cucumber, but the skin peels off and the interior is not unlike that of the watermelon, only finely flavoured and more luscious."

There is one serious flaw in this dense, multilayered book: there are almost no Jews in Teller's Old City. One chapter, about two-thirds of the way in, is set in the Jewish quarter, an area Teller finds different from everywhere else, with no cumin, no Arabic – and no Israeli checkpoints. The chapter focuses on the 1948 Jordanian conquest, when the Old City's Jewish inhabitants were evicted and their homes destroyed, and the 1967 Israeli conquest, when Israel bulldozed the Moroccan quarter to create the Western Wall Plaza. He interviews some Jewish residents who moved in after 1967. But after eighth-century banana-eating mystics, this feels a little meagre.

In an epilogue, Teller explains that he is not interested in balance, but rather in redressing the balance. "Jerusalem has many more sides than two, and many more quarters than the four that appear on its maps," he writes. But Israel is so powerful, its narrative so entrenched, and Teller wants to highlight the untold stories, so that they can be heard above the clamour. As he puts it, "This book rejects equality in favour of equity."

This might have been better explained in a prologue, so readers would know what to expect, but even so I feel it misses the point. Whatever a reader's politics – and mine happen to align with Teller's – it doesn't change the fact that the Jewish connection to Jerusalem long pre-dates the State of Israel. It deserves a more in-depth look in a serious book like this. Jewish stories would only have enriched this account. Their absence diminishes it.

Nine Quarters is a beautifully written and deeply researched book. But the curious reader will have to explore the Old City's Jewish history on their own. ≡

Jacob's ladder

Benjamin Balint

Professor of Apocalypse:
The Many Lives of Jacob Taubes
Jerry Z. Muller
Princeton University Press

"God is not bourgeois," said Jacob Taubes. Neither was Taubes, a brilliant interpreter of the ways in which politics is a continuation of religion by other means. A new biography, *Professor of Apocalypse*, by Jerry Muller, portrays an erratic enfant terrible who thrived on scandal, intrigue and disorder – a flouter of social proprieties and disciplinary boundaries alike. Muller renders a compelling portrait of "a wanderer between worlds", a man of inner disjunctions, poised "on the border between Judaism and Christianity, between scepticism and belief, between scholarly distance and religious fervor". But in tracing Taubes' fissured life – from Vienna to wartime Switzerland, from post-war New York to Jerusalem to Cold War Berlin – Muller gives us something larger: a final snapshot of the German–Jewish encounter, pulled into focus by a failed Jewish preacher to the gentiles.

Born in Vienna in 1923 into an illustrious rabbinic family, Taubes was educated in Switzerland, where he studied Talmud with Moshe Soloveitchik at the Montreux yeshiva and Protestant theology with Karl Barth in Basel. In his doctoral dissertation at the University of Zurich (the first and last book he would publish in his lifetime), Taubes surveyed messianic movements from the Hebrew Bible to nineteenth-century Marxism. "The pathos and the tremendous power of Marxist ideas," Taubes argued, "rest upon a theory of human salvation and the messianic vocation of the proletariat." In short, Marxists – not unlike the ideologists of the French and American revolutions – drew on religion as a source of utopian longing, in the attempt, Taubes said, to establish a "Kingdom of God – without God".

A couple of years after World War II ended, the 24-year-old Taubes escaped from the clutches of his traditionalist family to study at the Jewish Theological Seminary (JTS) in New York. One of his friends there, Richard L. Rubenstein (later to author the groundbreaking book *After Auschwitz: Radical Theology and Contemporary Judaism*), noticed "something indefinably disturbing, one might almost say demonic, about the man". Taubes seemed to care more about avoiding banality than cultivating rigour. He dismissed empirical social research as "*schmonzes*" (trifles), derided the "*schmalz*-theology of the nineteenth and twentieth centuries" and disdained "*Wissenschaft des Judentums* á la 3080 Broadway [the JTS address]" as a "fraud". He took a dim view of erudition for its own sake, especially if it slipped into "a kind of Ersatz of living". As his friend the Romanian-born philosopher Emil Cioran put it, "Taubes embodies a revulsion against every sort of dreary scholarship."

Taubes asked Leo Strauss, one of the German-born, Nazi-persecuted scholars at the "university in exile", New York's recently established New School for Social Research, to tutor him in Maimonides' teachings – or, more precisely, in Strauss's radical reading of esoteric meanings concealed in those teachings. Drawing on what he had absorbed from Strauss, Taubes led a decidedly undreary private seminar on Maimonides for the circle gathered around *Commentary* magazine, which included Daniel Bell, Nathan Glazer, Irving Kristol, Gertrude Himmelfarb, Milton Himmelfarb and Arthur A. Cohen. (Taubes made his first appearance in English in the pages of *Commentary*.) Kristol called Taubes "the only really charismatic intellectual" he had ever met.

Around this time, Susan Feldmann, the daughter of a renowned Hungarian psychoanalyst and granddaughter of a chief rabbi of Budapest, succumbed to Taubes' charisma. Her autobiographical novel *Divorcing* (reissued two years ago by New York Review Books Classics) describes a courtship that involved none of the usual dinner dates, movies or terms of endearment:

> [A] marriage that happened on the basis of a sermon he delivered to her alone on the evening they met and the next evening when she answered his marriage proposal by asking him to deflower her, the sermon and the proposal repeated for the next six weeks, always the same sermon delivered by the young rabbi from Vienna to the psychoanalyst's daughter who argued against God and marriage, till the night she could not answer him ...

In her letters, Susan addressed Jacob as her "my holy animal, my most trusted one, with whom I, a whorish pagan woman, made my eternal covenant". The couple transplanted their covenant to Jerusalem in autumn 1949. Before their departure, Taubes wrote to the philosopher Ernst Simon about the religious doubts that his close encounter with Strauss had evoked in him: "It is good to go to Eretz Yisrael and to test whether the ice of atheism and the cold aura that emanates from it will melt under the sun and fire of God's word."

In fact it was Taubes himself who melted under the scrutiny of his master, Gershom Scholem. At first enchanted by Taubes' luminous mind, the eminent scholar of Kabbalah soon wrote to Leo Strauss that his erstwhile protégé had produced little more than "rhapsodies on themes of others and hugely pretentious twaddle". In reply, Strauss remarked on Taubes' "shameless ambition". Hannah Arendt, who agreed with Scholem and Strauss on little else, likewise noted Taubes' talent for "bluffing people with Levantine cleverness".

In 1951, Scholem privately shared with Taubes devastating remarks about a psychologically ill student named Joseph Weiss, whose wife, Miriam, Taubes had seduced. When Taubes relayed those remarks to Weiss, Scholem accused Taubes of "an extreme breach of trust", severed contact and declared him persona non grata at the Hebrew University. (Such was Taubes' notoriety for indiscretion and treachery, Muller says, that colleagues who wished to spread a message would reveal it to Taubes in strictest confidence.) "Your disappointment is my greatest humiliation," Taubes replied to Scholem. For the rest of his life, his conversation with Scholem would be entirely one-sided, like a kind of marvellous soliloquy.

Banished from Jerusalem, Taubes landed on his feet at Harvard, where he taught courses on "the history of heresy" and Susan wrote her dissertation on the French philosopher and mystic Simone Weil. Four years later, Taubes got himself a professorship at

Columbia University. One of his students there, Morris Dickstein, said: "Radiating charm, intelligence, and mystery, Taubes drew men and women irresistibly into his orbit."

One of Taubes' closest relationships at Columbia was with Susan Sontag, who was his teaching assistant for three years. After they slept together, Sontag reported in her diary that he was "unexpectedly good + sensitive sexually". In her first novel, *The Benefactor* (1963), Sontag portrays Taubes as Professor Bulgaraux, a scholar of religious sects who speaks of "being liberated through contracting one's settled life and unleashing one's deepest fantasies". Sontag's then husband, Philip Rieff, was less taken by the conceit-laced man he described as "deeply sinister and evil".

Depending on who is asked, Taubes was a charismatic genius, a reckless charlatan, or both. Theodor W. Adorno charitably concluded that "there is part of him that really wants to do the right thing and that is exceptionally responsive, but that then some hard-to-control impulses get in the way ... This constellation leaves considerable characterological scars."

Muller makes no attempt to disguise his subject's scars: he neither excises nor excuses Taubes' philandering (including an affair with the Austrian author Ingeborg Bachmann, erstwhile lover of Paul Celan), his plagiarising (including from Scholem) or, most egregiously, what Muller calls his "almost animal-like instinct for human weakness and how to exploit it". A good biographer – especially of a character as polymorphously self-dramatising as Taubes – is not a stenographer. Rather than merely recount how others saw Taubes, Muller explores how Taubes saw himself.

Taubes increasingly identified with Paul of Tarsus, zealous apostle to the gentiles, whom Taubes regarded as "more Jewish than any Reform or liberal rabbi that I've encountered". Like Paul, Taubes felt torn (in Paul's phrase) between "Israel according to the flesh" and "Israel according to the spirit". And, following Paul, Taubes defined the Jewish people, bearers of a message both particular and universal, as "a *Volk* that is also a non-*Volk* (what a blessing!)". In universalising the Torah, Taubes said, Paul "drew heretical conclusions" from Jewish premises. "Just as the apostle unchained the content of Judaism into Christianity," Taubes told his friend Margarete Susman, "so I want to unchain this Christian content into something universal."

To cut the chains, Taubes honed the notion of "secularization", the translation of eschatology – descriptions of the end of history – into a this-worldly vernacular of modern politics. He wished thereby to catch "the political potential of theological metaphors". Modern politics – and the story it tells of increasing freedom and self-realisation – interprets and preserves traces of messianic longing. For Taubes, translating messianic motifs into practical politics begins with affirming that history has a fundamental direction, from creation towards redemption (however deferred). In the religious chronology that has its origins in the Hebrew Bible, history is not passively experienced as a cyclical succession of events; it moves towards some meaningful end and is thus subject to human action and responsibility. If we measure how the tides of history ripple with apocalyptic undercurrents, Taubes asserts, we would see that "the problem of time is a moral problem".

In the early 1960s, when he and Susan divorced, Taubes became an early academic jetsetter. After several years of commuting between New York and Germany, he moved to West Berlin in 1966 to serve as founding chair in Jewish studies at the

Free University, to marry a member of the Catholic aristocracy, Margherita von Brentano, and not least to explore a pressing question: how to live as a Jew in post-Shoah Germany. Just as he had approached Christianity as a Jew, now, equally unapologetically, he moved to Germany as a Jew. "The elements of my existence are discordant," Taubes confessed to a lover. "The circles of my language and my spirits, the Jewish and the German, confront one another today as two enemy brothers, as enemies to life and death, in a war without mercy, without reconciliation, and the slash goes right through me."

Taubes' German students from the "generation of 1968" welcomed his leftist cosmopolitanism and freewheeling style. "*Der Wunderrabbi*", as they nicknamed him, played to their desire to unburden themselves from the guilt of the Shoah their parents had perpetrated, and to their need for a "good Jew" – a descendant, figuratively speaking, of Paul and Marx. He became a hit in a way he had never been among Jews in New York or Jerusalem.

In turn, Taubes embraced German student radicals even as he rued their vilification of Israel. "Since the catastrophe of European Jewry," he declared in a radio talk, "the Jewish people grasps for a piece of land in Israel as a drowning man grabbing a plank. And whoever tries to knock this plank away continues – knowingly or unknowingly, wittingly or unwittingly – the Hitlerian fantasy and the methods of the Final Solution."

Life in Germany magnified Taubes' compulsions as a controversialist and contrarian. "I search for right-wing intellectuals of distinction to find a true opponent with the aid of whom one can ascend intellectually," he said. Just as he had once sought out Leo Strauss, Taubes now turned to Carl Schmitt, the "crown jurist" of the Third Reich. When he finally met Schmitt – whom he hailed as "still today the greatest mind in Germany" – Taubes said he felt awed by their "tremendous" (*ungeheuerlich*) conversations. Muller, who has previously written on German right-wing thinkers, observes dryly that "Taubes made Schmitt kosher for a leftist audience".

In his declining decades, Taubes led an ever more fractured life. In 1969, days after *Divorcing* got an unscrupulous and misogynistic review in the *New York Times*, Susan, aged forty-one, drowned herself off the Long Island shore. (Her body was identified by Susan Sontag.) Always mercurial, Taubes was diagnosed with bipolar disorder, and beginning in the mid-1970s he flitted in and out of psychiatric hospitals and consented to electroshock treatments. He found intermittent refuge in Paris, where he held court "like a Jewish Socrates", as the philosopher Babette Babich put it, and in Jerusalem, where he befriended stars of a younger generation, including Avishai Margalit, David Hartman, Guy Stroumsa and Moshe Halbertal. Leon Wieseltier, who met Taubes in Jerusalem in 1978, said he had lost nothing of his "narcotic relationship to religion".

Taubes was struck down by cancer and died in 1987, aged sixty-four. The decades since have sent resurgent waves of new readers not just to his dissertation, *Occidental Eschatology*, but to his posthumously published books: his essays, collected in *From Cult to Culture*, and his last lectures, *The Political Theology of Paul*.

"Taken from a great height," the German-Jewish cultural critic Siegfried Kracauer said of Taubes' teachings, "they remind one of aerial photographs; like these, they allow one to catch a glimpse of normally invisible configurations of the broader landscape they survey." An early mentor, warier of Jacob Taubes' soaring ambitions, cautioned the wunderkind against climbing too high: "In Jacob's dream, it is angels, and not men, who descend and ascend the countless steps … anyone who seeks to imitate them commits the most irreparable error." To its great credit, Muller's scintillating but earthbound biography makes no such mistake.

The unforgettable worlds of Natalia Ginzburg

Catherine Taylor

Works discussed:
The Little Virtues, translated by Dick Davis (Daunt, 2018)
Family Lexicon, translated by Jenny McPhee (Daunt, 2018)
The Road to the City, translated by Frances Frenaye (Daunt, 2021)
All Our Yesterdays, translated by Angus Davidson (Daunt, 2022)
The Dry Heart, translated by Frances Frenaye (Daunt, 2021)
Voices in the Evening, translated by D.M. Low (Daunt, 2019)
Happiness, as Such, translated by Minna Zallman Proctor (Daunt, 2019)
The Manzoni Family, translated by Marie Evans (Arcade Publishing, 2019)

In her 1949 essay "My Vocation", Natalia Ginzburg, with typical forthrightness and precision, describes her calling: "My vocation is to write and I have known this for a long time." Identifying the genesis of this vocation (*Il mio mestiere*, the original Italian title, literally means "my craft"), she explains:

> I had brothers who were much older than me and when I was small if I talked at table they always told me to be quiet. And so I was used to speaking very fast, in a headlong fashion with the smallest number of words, and always afraid that the others would start talking among themselves again and stop listening to me.

She discusses her prose style, with its frequent shifts between autobiography and fiction, and contends that all writing is shaped by "our personal happiness or unhappiness": "When we are happy our imagination is stronger; when we are unhappy our memory works with greater vitality." Ginzburg usually remains an impersonal observer, but here she alludes, briefly yet devastatingly, to the current of emotion that runs like a wound through her work: "After a time when I lived in the South I got to know grief very well – a real, irredeemable and incurable grief that shattered my life, and when I tried to put it together again I realised that I and my life had become something irreconcilable with what had gone before."

The "real, irredeemable and incurable grief" to which Ginzburg refers is the imprisonment, torture and murder, on 5 February 1944, of her husband, the Odesa-born Jewish anti-fascist activist and intellectual Leone Ginzburg, in the Nazi-controlled wing of the Regina Coeli prison in Rome. Her father had objected to the marriage, as he did to all his children's relationships, with performative annoyance: Leone was another "new star rising", Giuseppe Levi's term for any friend of his offspring he himself had not vetted.

Leone was thirty-four when he died, his widow twenty-seven. Faced with this loss, and with three young children to support, Ginzburg's vocation became her lifeline. In a richly evocative piece from the same collection, "Winter in the Abruzzi", Ginzburg writes about the period preceding Leone's death, when the family was exiled – both because of Leone's political allegiances and because they were Jews – from their home in the cosmopolitan northern industrial city of Turin to the tiny village of Pizzoli, some 80 kilometres south of Rome. Ginzburg draws a picture of the quixotic, quotidian life of a small Abruzzi village, its petty disagreements and shifting alliances, and the overwhelming homesickness of being exiled with the *contadini* (peasants) in "the vast, silent countryside and the motionless snow". This period, from 1940 to 1943, was marked by fear, frustration and incarceration for the family. And yet, as she notes at the end of the essay, after a few stark sentences on Leone's unbearable and lonely death the following year, "That was the best time of my life, and only now that it has gone from me forever – only now do I realise it."

*

Natalia Ginzburg was born Natalia Levi in Palermo, Sicily, on 14 July 1916, the second daughter and youngest of five children of Jewish histologist Giuseppe Levi and his Catholic wife, Lidia Tanzi. The family moved to Turin when Natalia was three, after her father accepted a professorship at the city's university. The Levis were a boisterous, intellectual, leftist, secular family, dominated by Giuseppe's idiosyncrasies and fiercely inflexible moods, anchored by Lidia's sunnier but no less eccentric personality. Ginzburg bottled this energy, the world of pre-fascist and, by 1927, fascist Italy in her heavily autobiographical novel *Family Lexicon*, awarded Italy's foremost literary prize, the Strega, in 1963.

By the early 1960s, Ginzburg was part of a cohort of mostly male writers who, collectively, represented the outstanding literary talents of the immediate post-war generation: Alberto Moravia, Primo Levi, Silvano Arieti, Elsa Morante, Cesare Pavese, Carlo Levi, Leonardo Sciascia, Giorgio Bassani and Italo Calvino. A number of these writers were, like Ginzburg, Jewish, or part-Jewish (Morante converted to Catholicism when she married Moravia in German-occupied Italy in 1941). Their shared anti-fascist stance and activities meant that most had at various times been imprisoned and forced into internal exile during the war – or worse, as in the case of Primo Levi, a chemist and member of the Italian Resistance also from Turin, who was deported to Auschwitz the same month Leone Ginzburg was murdered in Rome.

Primo Levi probably remains the most internationally renowned Italian writer of that generation. Ironically, as Marco Belpoliti recounts in *Primo Levi: An Identikit* (2022), his first book, *If This Is a Man*, was rejected by Pavese, editorial director at the publisher Einaudi, where Ginzburg worked as an editor after the war. Leone had been one of the founders of the publishing house, and after his death it became like a second family to her. It was on Ginzburg's recommendation that Levi's manuscript was sent to another publisher, eventually being published by Francesco de Silva in 1947. In an interview not long before his death in 1987, Levi said, "A book like mine, and like many others that came along after mine, was almost an act of rudeness, it was like spoiling a party."

Pavese was a catalyst for Ginzburg's own career, however. (In 1933, aged eighteen, Ginzburg had published her first short story, "I Bandini", in the magazine *Solaria*.) A decade later, Pavese, a close friend of Leone, wrote to Natalia while the family was in exile in the Abruzzi, exhorting her to "stop having children and write a novel that is better than mine". *The Road to the City* appeared in 1942, under the pseudonym Alessandra Tornimparte. Under the racial laws imposed in Italy in 1938, the year Natalia and Leone married, Jews were forbidden to publish. Ginzburg thus began her literary career engaged in the type of duality that marks her greatest work: the narrator as unsentimental bystander, writing complex and frequently chaotic situations and characters, all captured with an illusory simplicity.

In *The Road to the City*, rather than writing about her own precarious situation, Ginzburg recounts a bitter coming-of-age story that takes place in an impoverished rural community similar to the one where she had been exiled. Delia, a seventeen-year-old village girl from a big family, with a sporadically violent father and neglectful mother, yearns for the luxuries of the nearby big city, where she imagines becoming a different person, with fashionable "cork-soled shoes and the dress and the woven straw handbag". Her elder sister has escaped the dreariness of village life, "and my ambition was to do likewise". She starts going with one of her brothers and a cousin, Nini, who lives with them, along the dusty road to the city, "an hour's walk away", where each becomes their own mysterious city self: "When we got there we lost no time separating, as if we were total strangers." Nini soon finds a job in a factory. Delia falls in with wealthy Giulio, the local doctor's son, who takes her for a swim and ice cream: simple, childlike treats; but there is something more: "Then he took me to a hotel called the Moon. The hotel was at the end of a solitary street. With its drawn blinds and deserted garden it looked like a private house whose owners had gone away, but the rooms had mirrors and washbasins and rugs on the floor." The scene for both material and physical seduction is set, and when Delia gets pregnant, she and Giulio have to marry, though neither cares for the other. This is the surface of the novel: where Ginzburg excels is in its unexpected profundity. Naive and greedy for what she believes will constitute a happy life, Delia rejects her own feelings for Nini and his for her; by the end of the book's scant, serious 100 pages barely a year has passed, yet Delia has suffered all the world-weariness and losses of a much older woman.

Curiously, although published just under two years before Leone's death, the book's last lines seem to foretell that imminent tragedy: "It was harder and harder to remember the way he looked and the things he used to say, and it frightened me to think of him now that he had receded into the far distance and become one of the vast multitude of the dead."

Ginzburg was concerned all her life with the socio-economic and gender inequities of Italian society. A member of the Communist Party in the 1930s as well as the 1980s, she was elected to the Italian parliament as an independent in 1983. What she had witnessed during her years in Abruzzi remained with her – particularly the paltry options for women, whatever their class: "When I first arrived in that countryside," she wrote in "Winter in the Abruzzi", "all the faces looked the same to me, all the women, rich and poor, young and old resembled each other. Almost all of them had toothless mouths: exhaustion and wretched diet, the unremitting overwork of childbirth and breastfeeding, mean that women lose their teeth when they are thirty." Contrasting with this is Ginzburg's portrait in *Family Lexicon* of her mother, Lidia, whose "temperament was joyful ... my mother looked dry-eyed on the past's desolation and didn't mourn for it". (After the war, Lidia refused to support the communists, saying that "if Stalin came to take away my maid, I'd kill him".)

The harshness of women's lives and the fleeting youth of girls in particular are recurring themes in Ginzburg's narratives, something she shares with that phenomenon of twenty-first-century Italian literature Elena Ferrante. It seems apposite to mention Ferrante, since the inexhaustible interest in her books in recent years has prompted the anglophone world to further explore the supposedly "forgotten" Italian "woman writer". New York Review Books in the United States and Daunt Books in the United Kingdom have gone some way to slaking the thirst of avid readers of Ferrante who, having gorged on her Neapolitan tetralogy and other novels, have enthusiastically turned to Ginzburg's lemon-sharp, subtle plots and prose. Daunt has capitalised on this interest by reprinting and repackaging Ginzburg, with smart, thoughtful introductions by acclaimed contemporary writers including Rachel Cusk, Colm Tóibín, Claire-Louise Bennett and Tim Parks. The latest choice of endorser is a judicious one: the Irish writer Sally Rooney, global star of millennial literary fiction, has written the preface for Ginzburg's masterpiece, the novel *All Our Yesterdays*, first published in 1952 and reissued in 2022. "It was as if her writing was a very important secret I had been waiting all my life to discover," Rooney writes – a grandiose statement, but for many readers an assertion with which they can wholly identify.

Though it predates *Family Lexicon* by almost a decade, *All Our Yesterdays* reads almost as a companion piece to that book. In *Family Lexicon,* Ginzburg decided against pseudonyms for her characters, remarking in a brief introductory note that, "In the writing of this book I felt such a profound intolerance for any fiction, I couldn't bring myself to change the real names which seemed to be indistinguishable from real people." At almost 400 pages, *All Our Yesterdays* is long in comparison to Ginzburg's usual preference for brisk and bracing novellas. There is, as ever, a family at its core – or rather, two families, whose houses in a small northern town are situated across from each other, and whose lives become enmeshed in the years just prior to, during and straight after the war. In both, the domineering and tiresome patriarch is removed straightaway, leaving children of various ages and stages behind (and one nervous mother) plus venerable housekeepers and various servants – Ginzburg's family units always include these terrifically drawn ostensibly minor characters. Anna, the youngest of the family, is the book's key character, although, like Ginzburg herself in *Family Lexicon*, she is at first inconspicuous, her outline gradually filled in as time and circumstances evolve. Rooney describes her as "partial and contingent" in the preface. There is just one physical description of her in the entire book: "She was a plump girl, pale and indolent, dressed in a pleated skirt and faded blue pullover, and not very tall for her fourteen years."

Anna's eldest brother, Ippolito, now head of the family, their neighbour Emanuele, and the young men's friend Danilo are all covertly, and at this stage optimistically, involved in the anti-fascist movement, as were Ginzburg's own father, brothers, brother-in-law and future husband. Ingenuous as she is, Anna aspires also, at least in her imagination, to "revolution", but after a brief and indifferent liaison with Giuma, the younger son of the house opposite, she becomes pregnant just as war breaks out. The novel, which opens in languid, melancholic fashion – rather like Ginzburg's contemporary Giorgio Bassani's *The Garden of the Finzi Continis*, the ultimate elegy to the lost Jewish community of Ferrara – describes the experiences of ordinary individuals in a country in paralysis and under dictatorship. There is the suicide of an idealist, the incidental deaths of beloved minor characters (including an inherited dog) and the brutal awakening of Anna, who is saved by a fortuitous marriage to the older, richer Cenzo Rena and taken to his tiny village in the south. "The serious things of life," he informs her, "took you by surprise, they spurted up all of a sudden like water."

Here, among the squabbling villagers and internees, including four elderly Jews and some fledgling partisans, she hunkers down for the war's duration and the birth of her baby, against a backdrop of wolves howling in the pine woods in winter, the "wet and muddy" spring, the yellow dust of summer, and "the tomatoes laid out in front of houses to dry, for the making of tomato paste" that heralds autumn. Ginzburg is not a rhapsodic user of imagery, but there is something unforgettable about her portrayal of the Italian countryside, and its wartime food scarcity turns wood mushrooms, small green tomatoes and even a boiled egg sobbed over by an anxious girl into a visual feast.

Cenzo Rena's predictions about "the serious things of life" will prove tragically true. Vaguely dilettant when Anna first encounters him, he grows ever more unostentatiously heroic as the novel progresses. Ginzburg has been compared to Chekhov, one of her own favourite writers, yet in *All Our Yesterdays* there is more than a hint of Maupassant's tales about the valour of ordinary citizens caught up in war. It is also one of the few novels in which she fully develops Jewish fictional characters – along with the elderly village internees, there is the luckless, excitable Franz, a German Jew unhappily married to Emanuele's sister.

In an interview in later life (quoted in the 2021 *Tablet* article "Backyard Exiles" by Fredric Brandfon), Ginzburg, brought up assimilated and secular, says: "My Jewish identity became extremely important to me from the moment the Jews began to be persecuted. At that point I became aware of myself as a Jew." This identity, with its sense of ambivalence and apartness, echoes throughout her work, even though, as Tim Parks says in his introduction to *Family Lexicon*, "As a rule the way a character dresses gets more attention than his views on fascism." This is surely Ginzburg's point, though: both aspects can coexist in a person.

After the war Ginzburg returned to Turin, where her mother helped look after her children. She wrote a caustic, cold novel, *The Dry Heart* (1947), about a young woman who kills the older, manipulative man she has married to assuage her loneliness. It is almost cinematic in its immediacy and intensity. There is always the sense of someone missing in her writing, and that someone encompassed more than Leone: it was an entire generation lost to fascism and war. In *Voices in the Evening*, a series of linked stories published in 1961, the inhabitants of a small Italian town must deal, like the survivors of *All Our Yesterdays*, with a present drenched in recent memories – some of them insupportable – along with their past actions or inactions. As Colm Tóibín writes in his preface: "Ginzburg did not overdramatise the war in her writing, but sought to integrate it into her daily life: it seemed part of normality until it came close and then tore the lives of her characters asunder."

In 1950, there came a definitive and shocking event with echoes of the past. Cesare Pavese, Natalia and Leone's great friend and Natalia's mentor and colleague, committed suicide in a hotel room in Turin on 27 August, barely two weeks before his forty-second birthday. His best-known novel, *The Moon and the Bonfires*, was published two years later, the same year as Ginzburg's *All Our Yesterdays*: her novel contains a poignant depiction of a depressive man, an anti-fascist activist, who takes his own life. In the essay "Portrait of a Friend", a beautiful tribute to Pavese, Ginzburg writes (without naming him):

> And now it occurs to us that our city resembles the friend whom we have lost and who loved it; it is, as he was, industrious, stamped with a frown of stubborn feverish activity; and it is simultaneously listless and inclined to spend its time idly dreaming. Wherever we go in the city that resembles him we dream our friend lives again.

The same year, Ginzburg married her second husband, Gabriele Baldini, a professor of English literature. She kept the surname Ginzburg. The couple moved to Rome in 1952, and spent two years in England (1959–61) when Baldini was appointed director of the Italian Cultural Centre in London. They had two children in addition to Ginzburg's three with Leone, both disabled: a daughter born in 1954, and a son in 1959, who lived only a year. "He and I" is a spiky, affectionate essay about Ginzburg's relationship with Baldini and their marriage as they moved into middle age, which seemed very much one of opposites: he had once looked like "the actor Robert Donat" but now "resembled Balzac". Baldini died in 1969, leaving her widowed a second time, at the age of fifty-three.

In the late 1960s and for the next fifteen years Italy was again convulsed – from student revolts to strikes to terrorist attacks which killed hundreds. Ginzburg tracked the social and political impact of this period, known as the *Anni di Piombo* (Years of Lead), in her work. *Happiness, as Such* (1973) is an epistolary novel featuring a student, Michele, who, due to his affiliation with a radical group, has left his large family in Rome – including his dying father – for England. Michele is elusive, opaque, mainly fleshed out in the gossipy, pleading, angry and sad letters from his correspondents: his mother, sister, best friend, and the woman whose baby may or may not be his. As Claire-Louise Bennett comments in the book's introduction, the form of the novel "suited Ginzburg well, it allowed her to slide between a variety of 'I's' and to get right beneath the skin of each one". In the searching for Michele, who ultimately moves beyond anyone's means to control him, there is again the absence and yearning which is the core of Ginzburg's writing.

In 1987 Ginzburg was re-elected to parliament as a left-wing deputy. She concentrated on humanitarian issues, including lowering the price of bread, legal aid for victims of rape, and reform of the adoption laws. Disillusioned with party politics, she left parliament not long after. Her last major novel was a historical one: *The Manzoni Family* (1983), based on the life of a nineteenth-century man of letters, Milanese nobleman Alessandro Manzoni. It won the Bagutta Prize the year it was published. As ever, family and its complex ties were her subjects. In her final years more memoirs were published, and in 1999 Einaudi posthumously released the text of *It's Hard to Talk about Yourself*, a series for radio in which Ginzburg discussed her life and literary output.

Ginzburg died of cancer at home in Rome on 7 October 1991, aged seventy-five. No doubt she would have been alarmed to know that, in September 2022, a century after Mussolini's National Fascist Party came to power, a far-right bloc was elected to govern Italy. In the thirty years since her death, her renown has continued to grow: the reserved, stoical survivor and interpreter of the twentieth-century trauma of Italy, and specifically of Italy's Jews, who responded, as one of her characters in *Happiness, as Such* puts it, with works of "strange, icy, lonely consolation". ≡

Past issues

"For a long time now, the authority of knowledge has been under siege from those who march under the banner of pure belief."
—Simon Schama

The Return of History investigates rising global populism, and the forces propelling modern nativism and xenophobia.

"Traditional principles and allegiances have given way to realpolitik." —Lina Khatib

The New Middle East examines the dramatic changes unfolding in the region as new rivalries, blocs and partnerships are formed – based not on ideology but on pragmatism.

"The left has become the ideology that dare not speak its name." —Anshel Pfeffer

In *The Strange Death and Curious Rebirth of the Israeli Left,* Anshel Pfeffer takes the pulse of Israel's left wing, examining its health and prospects and dissecting the country's complex post-Netanyahu political reality.

Past issues

"If ink on paper can reassemble a world …"
—Rachel Kadish

The Jewish world of pre-war Europe was almost destroyed. If we hold up a lantern to that darkness, what can we discover about what was lost, what survived and what could have been?

"Younger writers were freed to think about specifically Jewish questions. [Their] work has a narrower appeal. Only time will tell if it is also a deeper one." —Adam Kirsch

After the Golden Age examines the current generation of leading American Jewish writers as they grapple with questions about religion, Israel, politics and multiculturalism.

"Iran's strategy is to eat away at American power, while legitimising its own role as a regional power with nuclear ambitions." —Kim Ghattas

Iran examines the motivations behind the country's changing role and influence in the Middle East, delving into the regime's secretive strategy and tactics.

Add these past issues to your subscription when buying online.

www.ingramcontent.com/pod-product-compliance
Lightning Source LLC
Chambersburg PA
CBHW030052170426
43197CB00010B/1498